Selected Poem

SELECTED POEMS
OF
VITTORIO SERENI

Chosen and translated by
Marcus Perryman & Peter Robinson

ANVIL PRESS POETRY

Published in 1990
by Anvil Press Poetry Ltd
69 King George Street London SE10 8PX

Copyright © Estate of Vittorio Sereni 1990
Translations and introduction
copyright © Marcus Perryman and Peter Robinson 1990

This book is published
with financial assistance from
The Arts Council

Designed and composed by Anvil
Photoset in Bembo by Wordstream
Printed in England
by Morganprint Blackheath Ltd

British Library Cataloguing in Publication Data

Sereni, Vittorio, 1913–1983
  Selected poems of Vittorio Sereni.
  I. Title   II. Perryman, Marcus   III. Robinson,
  Peter
  851'.912

ISBN 0 85646 204 7

ACKNOWLEDGEMENTS

The translators would like to thank Vittorio Sereni's literary executors for permission to publish these translations.

Peter Robinson received from the Judith E. Wilson Fund of the University of Cambridge English Faculty a travel grant which helped in the completion of an earlier manuscript.

Acknowledgements are due to the editors of the following, where some of these translations in earlier versions first appeared: *Argo, London Magazine, New Directions in Prose and Poetry 47* (New Directions, New York), *Numbers, PN Review, Siting Fires,* and especially to Alison Rimmer of the Cambridge Poetry Festival Society and John Welch of the Many Press for their help in the publication of *The Disease of the Elm and other poems* (Many Press, London 1983).

CONTENTS

INTRODUCTION / 11

FROM *Frontier* (1941)

Birthday / 33
Fog / 34
Storm at Salsomaggiore / 35
To M.L. Passing above her Town in an Express Train / 36
Diana / 37
Soldiers in Urbino / 38
3 December / 39
To Youth / 40
Winter in Luino / 41
Terrace / 42
Zenna Road / 43
September / 45
Your Memory in Me / 46
Creva Road / 47
See How the Voices Fall / 49

FROM *Algerian Diary* (1947)

Outskirts 1940 / 53
City at Night / 54
Bolognese Diary / 55
Belgrade / 56
Italian in Greece / 57
Dimitrios / 58
The Athenian Girl / 59
Algerian Diary / 61
The African Sickness / 73
September the Eighth / 77

FROM *The Human Implements* (1965)

Via Scarlatti / 81
Journey There and Back / 82
The Misapprehension / 83
On the Zenna Road Again / 84
Window / 86
The Sharks / 87
Years After / 88
Six in the Morning / 89
Discovery of Hatred / 90
Those Children Playing / 91
Saba / 92
Passing / 93
Situation / 94
The Friends / 95
Appointment at an Unusual Hour / 96
In Sleep / 98
The Lines / 102
The Alibi and the Benefit / 103
Poetry is a Passion? / 104
A Dream / 107
On the Creva Road Again / 108
On a Cemetery Photograph / 110
To a Childhood Companion / 111
From Holland / 113
The Wall / 115
The Beach / 117

FROM *Variable Star* (1981)

Those Thoughts of Yours of Calamity / 121
In an Empty House / 122
Place of Work / 123
Works in Progress / 124
Interior / 127

Of Cuts and Stitches / 128
Revival / 129
Giovanna and The Beatles / 130
Each Time that Almost / 131
Niccolò / 132
Nocturne / 134
Madrigal to Nefertiti / 135
Requiem / 136
First Fear / 137
Second Fear / 138
Other Place of Work / 139
The Disease of the Elm / 140
Uphill / 142
In Parma with A. B. / 143
Autostrada della Cisa / 145
Rimbaud / 147
Progress / 148
Another Birthday / 149

NOTES / 151

Introduction

VITTORIO SERENI was born on 27 July 1913 in Luino, a small town on Lake Maggiore near the Swiss border. The poet's earliest memory, recalled in an interview from 1969,[1] was the news in May 1915 that Italy had entered the First World War. Sereni also said he clearly remembered word reaching Luino of the defeat at Caporetto in October 1917. This defeat and a subsequent sense of national shame contributed to the rise of fascism, which resulted, after the March on Rome, in Benito Mussolini's achievement of power in 1922. Sereni's father, a customs official, was an early member of the Luino fascist party. However, two years later, in 1924, after the murder of the socialist deputy Matteotti, his father left the party in protest. The following year he was transferred to Brescia, and there Vittorio Sereni completed his secondary education.

Sereni started writing poetry at the age of sixteen. When in 1933 the family moved again, this time to Milan, he began to make literary friendships. He attended Milan University and there met his future wife, Maria Luisa Bonfanti. Sereni had intended to study law, but changed to literature, and in 1936 graduated with a thesis on the poet Guido Gozzano (1883–1916). At university he came under the influence of the philosopher Antonio Banfi, and was involved with a circle of young writers and critics, including the poet Antonia Pozzi, whose suicide at the age of twenty-six in 1938 prompted Sereni's poem '3 December'.

Among his early poetic influences were the Ungaretti of *L'allegria* (1931) and *Sentimento del tempo* (1933), poems from Quasimodo's *Ed è subito sera* (1942), and, above all, Eugenio

Montale, whose *La Casa dei Doganieri e altri versi* had appeared in 1932. Sereni also absorbed the lessons of French Symbolism, but his own original and authentic note was audible from the first. In 1937, the poet Carlo Betocchi introduced readers to a new young poet by publishing two of Sereni's poems in *Frontespizio*. He helped to found and became a co-editor of the literary magazine *Corrente*, and began contributing to a number of others including the Florentine *Letteratura* and *Campo di Marte*. Florence was at this time the centre of activities for the Hermeticist poets, who included Ungaretti and Montale. Vittorio Sereni was not part of this group, but has been variously linked with it. He, however, emphasized his difference, describing himself as very much to one side of Hermeticism.[2]

During the next two years, Sereni completed his compulsory military service, and trained as a school teacher, working for a short time in Modena. The wider historical context of these years, and of Sereni's early poetry, is characterized by Mussolini and Ciano's ever more disastrous foreign policy. The invasion of Abyssinia in 1935 led to sanctions against Italy led by Great Britain and the League of Nations. Italian regiments fought on Franco's side in the Spanish Civil War. In 1938 Mussolini signed the Pact of Steel with Hitler's Germany, and finally in the summer of 1940 brought Italy into the Second World War, expecting to profit from a speedy Nazi victory.

On 19 June 1940, Vittorio Sereni married Maria Luisa Bonfanti, a student of literature and a native of Parma. Their eldest daughter, Maria Teresa, was born on 24 July 1941. In the same year Sereni published his first book of poems. *Frontiera* was printed by Corrente in an edition of three hundred and twenty copies. An enlarged edition, retitled *Poesie*, was issued by Vallecchi in 1942. It contained an author's note in which the poet explained that he had changed the title from the 'more cherished and precise one' of the first edition because, at that point in the war, his one volume of poems might come to be his only book, and he therefore felt the need to give it a form which could prove definitive. The note, dated August 1942 and deriving from the time when Sereni believed he was about to be posted to North Africa, concludes: 'This is why, at the moment that he leaves for remote parts, and his fate as a living creature is placed in the balance, he wishes to entrust his book once more to the heartfelt memory of his friends.'[3]

2

The title *Frontiera* has been variously interpreted: it is the geographical border between Italy and Switzerland; it is the frontier that marks the end of youth and, as in Joseph Conrad's *The Shadow-Line* to which Sereni's early poems have been compared,[4] the border separating the living from the dead. It is also the line, about to be crossed, between the precarious peace of the thirties and another world war. The presence of these frontiers adds implications to what Franco Fortini has called Sereni's effort to 'reduce as much as he can his own visual field',[5] for it is in the nature of a frontier both to focus tension and be on the periphery. A frontier also marks the point where an 'elsewhere' beckons and threatens. It can even be the line across which a fidelity to the poet's inner impulse, and fidelity to the objects of vision must be negotiated. Writing in 1940, Sereni praised Montale's second book, *Le occasioni* (1939), for a distinctive type of poem 'faithful to its actual earthly origins, to the difficulties that shaped it, to the occasions that have favoured it'; later, he describes the space of the text as 'an enchanted limit within which things may truly exist'.[6]

The acknowledgement of limits, and the danger involved in crossing them, gives to Sereni's early poetry a quietly voiced political dimension, implicitly opposed to the self-aggrandizing rhetoric of d'Annunzianism in fascist Italy.[7] Yet the frontier is also alluring in these poems, and their elegiacally idyllic tone transforms ambivalent circumstances into a romance of mild aesthetic pleasure. Their resistance is a form of perplexity. As Montale commented in an essay of 1965, 'The young poet hesitates on the threshold of poetry in a season which is not propitious for poetic compositions in a high key';[8] while Franco Fortini more acerbically noted that 'without the war and Italy's defeat Sereni would scarcely have emerged from the limitations of an educated belles-lettres-ism.'[9]

'Soldiers in Urbino', a poem from the time of Sereni's pre-war military service, concludes with a sudden shock delivered to the wistful, wandering soldiers by the distant sounds of lorries. In 'Terrace' a torpedo-boat on Lake Maggiore looking for contraband, but ominously war-like, catches the poet and his companions in its searchlight. When the vessel goes away at the poem's end, it leaves behind feelings both of relief and abandonment. Such fleeting encounters in these poems foreshadow a more harrowing scrutiny, as in 'September' where 'Through already certain death / we will walk with more courage ...'. *Frontiera* is also a volume of studies in transitory beauty, friendship and love. The poet appears to be emerging into his own in an idyllic landscape, but one doomed to come to grief. In his 1966 note to the definitive third edition, Sereni called it 'my pre-war book, but with one foot already in the war – as can be seen, I believe, not only from the dates.'[10]

3

In the autumn of 1941, Sereni, an infantry lieutenant, became part of a draft intended to reinforce the armies in North Africa. The next eighteen months of his life consisted of postings from one place to another, always with the prospect of becoming a casualty in the war against first the British and then the Allies in Libya and Egypt. His war was, in fact, a prolonged postponement of battle. After a sojourn in Bologna during the winter and spring of 1941–2, Sereni was sent by troop train through the Balkans to Greece. Four months were passed in Athens during the summer of 1942, expecting to join Rommel's advancing armies. Then Sereni was returned to Italy in the autumn, the war in Egypt turning definitively against the Axis forces after El Alamein.

Even in early 1943, Sereni and his fellow soldiers expected to be sent to support the retreating forces on the other Mediterranean shore. April saw his regiment transported to Sicily as part of the coastal defences in preparation for anticipated Allied landings from the sea at Trapani, on the western side of the island. However, on 24 July, the eve of Mussolini's fall from power, and two weeks after the initial landings in Sicily, American forces arrived at Trapani from the landward side and the Italian troops, with little reason left to save face, surrendered almost without a shot being fired. Sereni's prose accounts of these events make it clear that there was barely any will to resist. The Sicilians, far from sympathetic to the fascist régime, were encouraging the soldiers to surrender or desert; the chain of military command was in shreds to the highest levels; and morale was, understandably, not good. There was desertion, but also a prevalent air of fatalistic passivity. Writing twenty-six years later, Sereni describes a sense of culpability in that state of mind: 'fate, we say, or else chance; on the contrary, it's the point at which a lengthy inertia unconscious of itself is released and becomes a precipitous slide'.[11]

During the summer of 1943, Sereni and the other prisoners of war were transferred to North Africa. The poet was in Oran on 8 September 1943, aboard a ship which would have taken him to a prison camp in America, when General Badoglio's government signed a separate armistice with the Allies. This crucial moment in Italy's history is alluded to in the poems 'September the Eighth' and 'In Sleep'. The consequences of Badoglio's armistice were that Italy was occupied by the German armies in the North and the invading Allies in the South. Badoglio's broadcast gave no other order to Italian soldiers than to defend themselves against attack from any side. Thus they were left with three choices: to go into hiding, attempt to support the fascists, or form anti-fascist partisan groups. The Germans made immediate reprisals against the Italians.

Italian prisoners of war were required to state whether they were loyal to Badoglio, and, if not, were considered under a different category. This placed Sereni and those like him in the unusual position of being the prisoners of powers who had created a 'co-belligerency' status for Italy. Sereni was not shipped to America, but spent the next two years in various POW camps in Algeria and French Morocco. In the autumn of 1943 Mussolini, rescued by German paratroops, was installed in a puppet republic at Salò on Lake Garda. There ensued a Civil War in which the German forces and fascist militias were first harassed and then defeated by partisans supplied and partly co-ordinated by the Allies. Excluded from the experience of the Resistance by his capture and imprisonment, Sereni, like his fellow prisoners of war, was left on the edge of a decisive historical moment; yet this condition itself constituted a part of Italy's history. Added to the frontier in Sereni's first book, this historical periphery further confirms Giovanni Raboni's observation that 'The centrality of Sereni's poetry significantly derives from an initial marginality.'[12]

4

Diario d'Algeria was published by Vallecchi in 1947. The previous year, Sereni had been awarded a Libera Stampa Prize *ex aequo* with Umberto Bellintani for his then unpublished work. Sereni's second book of poems bears witness to the wartime experiences of deferral and enforced absence. The 'love romance just caught sight of' in 'Belgrade', the 'irreparable time / of our cowardice' in 'Bolognese Diary', or the poet's identification in 'Dimitrios' and 'The Athenian Girl' with young Greeks surviving under Axis occupation form tender resistances to the Europe of 1942.

Sereni personifies the continent in 'Italian in Greece', calling upon a Europe watching over him as he descends 'unarmed and absorbed / in my slender myth amid the ranks of the brutal'. Franco Fortini took issue with these lines in an epigram, 'Sereni slender myth', of 1954: 'You ask pardon of the "ranks of the brutal" / if you want to leave them. Give up that tired / and bloody game of modesty and pride.'[13] It is a criticism of Sereni's gentility, his absence of overt political commitment, to which the poet later replied,[14] and which is deflected by Leonardo Sciascia's comment that 'There is evidently still in Sereni the sense of Europe's fragility ... but also an idea of Europe as *other* than the war, the violence, the Nazi-fascism. An idea, a myth, a utopia ...'.[15]

When the idea of Europe returns in the fourth part of 'Algerian Diary', it invokes both the political map of June 1944, the D-Day landings, and that utopia of peace and culture to which Leonardo Sciascia referred. Sereni calls upon the first soldier dead on the Normandy beaches to pray for Europe if he can, because, the poet admits, 'I am dead to war and to peace'. His isolation in North Africa leaves him unable to respond; yet in the statement itself Sereni registers a vitality, alive to the continent's fate, belying the location of the poem, Camp Hospital 127, where he was recovering from fever.

The twelve poems of 'Algerian Diary' shape the period of a year into a purgatorial expiation for passive complicity. The aggravated inner divisions of Sereni's position are expressed, as Fortini has noted, in 'an anger without object, beneath the appearance of perplexity and stupefaction.'[16] Yet also audible in these poems of such unpropitious circumstances is a mitigating, a sustaining tenderness towards loved ones at a distance, and a celebration of the gifts and talents, the resourcefulness of fellow prisoners. The sequence's tone nurtures by example virtues opposed to the conditions it must face. By a persistent and, as it was to prove, a consistent fidelity to the given occasions, Sereni's work rejects simplifying certainties and, glimpsing possibilities of personal and cultural gladness, refuses to be overwhelmed.

5

Vittorio Sereni was returned to Italy in 1945, and took up teaching again, now in Milan. From 1952 to 1958 he worked in the publicity department of Pirelli. These were also the years in which Sereni's parents died (his father in December 1952, his mother in 1958) and the Serenis' other two daughters were born: Sylvia on 12 June 1947 and Giovanna on 22 June 1956. The family spent its summers at Bocca di Magra, a holiday resort on the Ligurian coast which soon after the war became the summer residence for various members of the Italian literary community, including Elio Vittorini, Franco Fortini, and the publisher Giulio Einaudi. Many of Sereni's poems in his last two books are set in Bocca di Magra.

In 1958, Sereni changed his job a final time, joining Mondadori as literary director. He made annual visits to the Frankfurt Book Fair, from which his prose fiction *L'Opzione* (The Option) draws its inspiration. It was first published in 1964, and then again in the 1980 volume *Il sabato tedesco* (The German Saturday). Through his position at Mondadori, his works and literary conduct, Sereni had a decisive influence on the direction of Italian poetry in the sixties and seventies. His contemporary Giorgio Caproni has described him as 'a sure guide, and we may also say a sure master, for a numerous group of young poets, who, through his example have then discovered each his own proper personality.'[17]

Sereni did not publish his third book of poetry until 1965. *Gli strumenti umani* (The Human Implements) thus covers a period of twenty years, spanning the post-war reconstruction of Italy as well as its industrial and consumer transformation, the 'economic miracle' of the fifties and sixties, under various coalitions of the centre-left, excluding the Communists. In 1946 the house of Savoy, the royal family of Risorgimento Italy, was voted into exile by referendum, and a republic formed. On 18 April 1948, a date alluded to in the poem for Umberto Saba, the Christian Democrats defeated the Communists and Socialists in the first elections of the new republic. Saba described this outcome as a 'dictatorship of the priests', and in a letter to him of 23 April 1951, Sereni wrote 'I remember the time you were here, a dusty time of things in ruins, of things that wanted to be born and quickly died – and through these your figure moved, like a pilgrim's, coming from far too different countries.'[18] A sense of political frustration felt by many Italians was combined in Sereni with a belief that the ideals of those who fought the partisan war from which he was excluded had been betrayed by the political compromises that formed the basis for the years of prosperity.

'In Sleep', written in 1963 but exploring the atmosphere of 1948–53, gives specific contexts in work, sport, music and love for the poet's thoughts of guilt, his suspicions that the course of life has been 'deviated down false tracks', as Sereni writes in 'Those Children Playing'. The hidden wound in the last part of 'In Sleep', in 'Appointment at an Unusual Hour', and expressed at the conclusion to 'Saba' rebukes the contemporaneity which Sereni's continuing commitment to a poetry of occasions and objects obliges him stubbornly to record. Once more, the poet's only acceptable weapon is a sense of joy, a gift for friendship and the need to foster love. 'Years After' concludes: 'Then do not turn away love I beg you / and friendship remain and defend us.'

Another poem, 'The Friends', exemplifies the reassurance and help that 'Years After' calls for. In a prose note, 'On the Back of a Piece of Paper', Sereni writes of 'The Friends' that 'The people mentioned by name in these lines, by their actual names, are alive and real ...'.[19] He fears that even thanking them by name in a poem he may have reduced them to a literary pretext. Much of Sereni's work is similarly situated on the difficult and shifting territory where each composition is an independent aesthetic fact, and also a contextualized addressed utterance. 'On the Back of a Piece of Paper' is one of the many diaristic comments, autobiographical sketches, pieces of literary criticism, translations and self-analyses collected in *Gli immediati dintorni* (The Immediate Surroundings), first published in 1962 and reissued in an enlarged edition in 1983.

Massimo Grillandi has noted that the years in which Sereni's third book was patiently being composed were characterized by the call for a poetry determined to express and advance its position in relation to the individual and society.[20] The neo-realism of the forties and fifties gave way to a wave of avant-garde experimentalism. In this context, poems such as 'The Lines', 'Poetry is a Passion?' and 'A Dream' exemplify Sereni's disinclination to answer appeals for overt political commitment, or poetry written to fit any form of ideological or aesthetic programme. The influence of Benedetto Croce's concept of intuition as the foundation of art can be detected here, and Sereni makes reference to the philosopher in a published letter to Charles Tomlinson, where he praised the English poet for being free of 'any preconstituted understanding' and continued 'In you understanding is an outcome, a crowning of the specific experiment, it forms with the formation of the poem.'[21]

The disinclination to be bound by categories or theories also accounts for Sereni's resistance to the title of poet. In 'Self-Portrait', a prose note from 1978, he describes how he sees himself in the face of what he has written: 'with reluctance, derived from the discomfort of going about with the title of writer and, more specifically, of poet, a designation which there's nothing to be ashamed of, but which disturbs me as soon as I think of that separated corps, the inexorably fenced-off zoo which ... the writers' and, in particular, the poets' world has become.'[22] Nonetheless, *Gli strumenti umani* is a book with a deep and wide cultural allusiveness, from the quoted snatches of a popular song in the final part of 'In Sleep' to the enigmatic citation of a statement by Leonardo da Vinci in 'On a Cemetery Photograph'. In the author's note to the book, Sereni observed of the many 'verses or phrases taken from living or dead authors and inserted at times in the text without quotation marks or italics' that 'They should be recognizable as and when they occur, and it is therefore superfluous to state both where and why they are included.'[23] By these various reluctances Sereni hoped to sustain a sense of the naturalness of poetic composition, and was defending his own creative impulse against the dangers of distortion presented by literary, economic and political currents in the intellectual life of his immediate surroundings.

Giuliano Dego, however, thought that the 'loud, empty call of some of the avant-garde had distracted Sereni from his true nature'.[24] There is certainly a decisive development in the poet's language and style. He moves from the stunned and piercing post-war lyrics, such as 'Journey There and Back', to 'On the Creva Road Again' or 'The Wall', longer reflective monologues or colloquies which draw upon narrative qualities and Dantescan encounters with rebarbative voices. Eugenio Montale catches the distinctive paradox of reluctance and persistence in Sereni's work when he observes that the poet, accepting 'the necessity of camouflaging oneself beneath the *modus vivendi* of the man on the street', achieved a style which, while it 'should logically lead to silence, is nevertheless obliged to be eloquent'.[25] Sereni remained faithful to his inner impulse and prevented it from drying up by absorbing its opposite, the literary and socio-political opposite of his tender lyricism, 'his true nature'. *Gli strumenti umani* was published by Einaudi in 1965, the year in which Sereni received the Montefeltro Prize at Urbino. In the same year, he produced a new edition of *Diario d'Algeria* with Mondadori, and in 1966 Vanni Scheiwiller issued a new edition of *Frontiera*, thus giving a definitive shape to thirty years of poetry.

7

Vittorio Sereni writes of himself as recently dead and returned to haunt his own house in 'Six in the Morning', and in 'Passing' he asks, 'Am I already dead and come back here?' A revenant in post-war Italy, the poet's early preoccupation with the presence of the dead among the living is refocussed to define the survival of wounding experience into a world that has not shared, or has too soon forgotten or actively concealed the suffering endured. The final poem of *Gli strumenti umani*, 'The Beach', ends with the affirmation that the dead will speak. Sereni had said of himself in 1944 that he was dead to war and to peace, yet, despite their ever more continuous preoccupation with mortality, his later works are an extended meditation upon the dangers and possibilities of becoming dead to life.

Interviewed by Giuliano Dego for the *London Magazine*, Sereni said, 'I find myself falling into ways of thought like those which perplexed me during the war, and even more frantic, more confused. I feel the same sense of emptiness, of despair as I felt then, not knowing what to do with myself...'.[26] Sereni had visited the United States two years before this, in 1967, a journey which prompted 'Works in Progress'. He made two trips to Egypt, in 1973 and 1979, and also visited China in 1980. These were years in which his literary stature was reaffirmed by awards of the Antonio Feltrinelli Prize for poetry in 1972, and, four years later, the Monselice Prize for translation. His selected poems, *Poesie scelte 1935–1965* edited by Lanfranco Caretti, was published by Mondadori in 1973 and, in the same year, Liviana Editrice in Padova issued a selection of critical essays, *Letture preliminari* (Preliminary Readings).

Perhaps most significant of his journeys was the 1969 return to Sicily on holiday with his wife and youngest daughter. From this came *Ventisei* (Twenty-Six), a prose work first published in 1970 and reprinted in the 1987 Scheiwiller volume *Senza l'onore delle armi* (Without the Honour of Arms), a collection of prose writings about his capture and imprisonment. In *Ventisei* Sereni attempts to bring himself through his debilitating memories and recurrent images of war, to dissociate himself from irrational fears and gnawing desires for an experience unlived. By living the events again, transformed in writing, he seeks to resolve his self-division, his isolation from others, and even to put his impulse to write behind him: 'Why besides having a body, a gaze, and a voice, are we not endowed with a special transparency which allows those close to us to live with us fully, without recourse to that distorted emanation of ourselves which writing is, and to which we regularly refer them?'[27] It is the confrontation of this wish in writing, a self-perpetuating contradiction, which provides one of the impulses for Sereni's last poetic phase.

8

Numerous echoes of *Ventisei* occur in the poems of Sereni's last book, *Stella variabile* (Variable Star). The emblematic 'trees we'll leave to die' of the prose are intensified and concentrated in 'The Disease of the Elm'. Similarly, the narrative concludes, 'There stands before me a wood, the words, to travel through following a line that gradually forms as you walk, forward (or back) towards the transparency, if that is the right word for the future.'[28] This 'transparency' also figures in the 'horror of that emptiness' in the poem 'In Parma with A.B.' (addressed to the poet Attilio Bertolucci), and in the 'colour of nothingness', the final line of 'Autostrada della Cisa'. The conclusion of *Ventisei* also reaffirms Sereni's impulse, present too in these last poems, always to move by transforming the material of memory towards experiencing the world afresh.

Yet this transparency, emptiness and nothingness indicates how, while the moral basis for social and political analysis in *Gli strumenti umani* remains, the grounds of the encounter have shifted into a more metaphysical realm. 'In an Empty House' makes reference to the Munich Crisis of September 1938, regarded by some in Italy at the time as a diplomatic triumph for Mussolini. Sereni adopts it as an instance not only of personal culpability, but of evil itself in the world. Similarly, the occasions of friendship in Sereni's earlier work have become, with *Stella variabile*, encounters with absent because dead friends. In the poem 'Niccolò', set in Bocca di Magra, Sereni calls upon the literary critic Niccolò Gallo to 'stay with me, you like it here, / and heed me, you know how.'

In *Gli strumenti umani*, Sereni sought to remain true to his poetic impulse by confronting and absorbing its opposite, the world of industrial transformation, of European economic opportunism and convenient political amnesia. The authentic impulse is set at risk by this process, and risks being repressed or incapacitated by the opposing material it seeks to absorb. The nature of this dilemma, or better, condition of writing for Sereni helped to determine the shape of *Stella variabile*, which was published by Garzanti in December 1981, and won the Viareggio Prize the following year.

A variable star is one whose brightness varies periodically, does not maintain the same apparent size in the sky. It is, as it were, the opposite of Keats's 'Bright star! would I were steadfast as thou art – '. The alternating intensity of the light signifies the poet's movement between creative 'impotence and potentiality', between what Sereni called his 'difficulties in understanding the world and the continuing impulse to discover new and hidden significances'.[29] He calls upon the variable star in 'The Disease of the Elm' to guide him as long as it can: a further significance of the changing degrees of brightness is a wavering between the enchanting and flattering appearances of life and the alluring transparency, the emptiness which is death.

In a 1972 interview with Massimo Grillandi, Sereni observed that 'There's an age at which we begin to know with certainty that one day we will die. Before this, whoever writes poetry is only paying court to death. I include myself, you understand. When one enters into that certainty, one tends to name death much less.'[30] In *Ventisei* and *Stella variabile* the presence of death, albeit unnamed, dominates the concluding pages. Talking to Ferdinando Camon, Sereni said about his position regarding the conflicting claims of aesthetic styles and political attitudes: 'Above all I believe in dialogue.'[31] In his last book the conversation is, as Maurizio Cucchi reviewing *Stella variabile* wrote, a 'no longer interrupted colloquy with death'.[32] The attempt to come into relation with another presence in Sereni's poetry enacts its search for truth. The words of others in the poems set them at risk, even challenge their right to exist. Sereni's work is in turn brought to self-definition by its relation to the voices which oppose it.

'Autostrada della Cisa' invokes Petronius's sybil who 'more and more wishes to die', also adopted as epigraph to *The Waste Land*. Sereni attempts in his poem once more to initiate a meeting. Driving through the alternating brightness and darkness of tunnels on the motorway, he writes 'I extend a hand. It returns to me empty. / I reach out an arm, embrace a shoulder of air.' Yet by a familiar paradox, the resignation to approaching death, the realization that you are about to leave and not return gives a sudden final vividness to the apprehended world. Reading the last poems of Vittorio Sereni invites and fosters a refreshed relation to life. In the prose 'Self-Portrait', Sereni notes of his impulse that 'It lives, if it lives, on a contradiction from which filters, on and off, a primary (call it deluded, call it unfulfilled, call it unrequited) love of life.'[33]

9

Sereni died of heart failure on 10 February 1983, and was buried in Luino on the following day. *Tutte le poesie*, the collected poems, edited by the poet's eldest daughter Maria Teresa, was published posthumously by Mondadori in June 1986. It contained, as well as the four books which constitute Sereni's poetic œuvre, a reprint of *Il musicante di Saint-Merry* (The Musician of Saint-Merry), first published by Einaudi in 1981, a selection of Sereni's translations from the Orphée Noir, Pound, Char, Williams, Frénaud, Apollinaire, Camus, Bandini and Corneille.

Concluding his review of *Il musicante di Saint-Merry*, Franco Fortini cited lines from René Char's prose poem 'Rémanence' (Retentivity): ' "What do you suffer from? / From the unreal intact within the devastated real" ... I believe poems are

25

written, and are translated, as an irrevocable response, as much to that question as to its reply.'[34] Sereni suggested one response by quoting in his introduction to the translations a remark of Sergio Solmi's: 'The translation is born, in contact with the foreign text, with the force, the irresistibility of the original inspiration. At its birth presides something like an impulse of envy, a complaint at having lost the irrecoverable lyric occasion, at having left it to a more fortunate brother poet in another language.'[35] While envy can be creatively inhibiting, it may also, through translation, impel a writer to counteract its influence by finding, in the irreducibly different experiences of other poets' lyric occasions, analogous solutions to comparable [sufferings.]

Sereni suffered the loss of an irrecoverable lyric occasion by his imprisonment in North Africa during 1943–5. He states in his introduction that 'I had never thought of translating the work of others until a fellow prisoner, who read English much better than I did but who had no experience in writing poetry, gave me his literal version of a poem by E. A. Poe, asking me to make an Italian poem of it ...'. He quotes from memory the first two lines of his lost translation of 'The Conquering Worm', noting that they seemed to 'be in accord with the particular situation and state of mind in which we found ourselves then ...'.[36] Sereni tells the story to imply something of his own compulsion in translating, a desire to overcome isolation, to discover our own true limits in relation to others. He translated extensively from René Char, including the complete *Feuillets d'Hypnos*, published by Einaudi in 1968. Rendering these prose poems related to Char's experience in the Resistance may have helped to assuage the wound of 'In Sleep' and 'Appointment at an Unusual Hour'.[37] The inclusion of Sereni as translator in his versions of Char, in the process of remembrance and transformation, works to convert the envy of another's lyric occasions into a living gratitude.

One of the times we met Vittorio Sereni, discussing an ambiguous word with no equivalent ambiguity in English, he suggested a rule for translating him which we have followed as far as possible: to render the most apparent, even the most banal meaning. We have translated literally wherever feasible, but in certain cases the registers of a literal version would have produced an intolerably discordant English text. In all instances, however, literally or not, we have done our best to be faithful to the original poem.

Wishing to imitate the poetic nature of Sereni's verse, we have kept as close to the number of lines, the syntax and the format of the Italian as has been possible in another language. Rhymes, metre, the texture of an original poem are largely left behind in translating; whenever, by chance and good fortune, the English language allowed and suggested comparable poetic devices, we have adopted them to supply the loss and give some impression of Sereni's technical sensitivity, delicacy and originality. The language of poetry intimately resembles but is not identical to the speech of every day. We have wanted to convey Sereni's distinctiveness in Italian, and have not tried to naturalize his sensibility in our language. Our translations are thus, we hope, poems in English, rather than English poems.

The translations published here are the result of many hours of illuminating, educative and pleasurable collaboration. We hope that some of our love for Vittorio Sereni's work is conveyed to the reader in what follows. Conversations with many people in England and Italy have been invaluable. We would like to thank Maria Teresa Sereni for the help she has given us, and the hospitality that she and her family have always shown. Above all, for his friendly encouragement, guidance and understanding, we owe a deep debt of gratitude to Vittorio Sereni.

MARCUS PERRYMAN
PETER ROBINSON

September 1988

Notes

1. Giuliano Dego, 'A Poet of Frontiers' in *London Magazine* vol. 9 no. 7, October 1969, p. 38.
2. Massimo Grillandi, *Vittorio Sereni* (Florence, 1972) p. 2.
3. Both citations from Vittorio Sereni, *Tutte le poesie* edited by Maria Teresa Sereni (Milan, 1986) p. 59.
4. Carlo Muscetta, in *Rinascita*, November–December 1947, and cited in Vittorio Sereni, *Poesie scelte 1935–1965* edited by Lanfranco Caretti (Milan, 1973) p. xxix.
5. Franco Fortini, *Saggi italiani* 1 (Milan, 1987) p. 125 and translated by Gavin Ewart in *Italian Writing Today* ed. Raleigh Trevelyan (Harmondsworth, 1967) p. 153.
6. Vittorio Sereni, *Letture preliminari* (Padua, 1973) pp. 9, 11.
7. See Maria Laura Baffoni Licata, *La poesia di Vittorio Sereni* (Ravenna, 1986) p. 50.
8. Eugenio Montale, *Sulla poesia* (Milan, 1976) p. 330 and translated by G. Singh in Eugenio Montale, *Selected Essays* (Manchester, 1978) p. 93.
9. Fortini, op. cit. p. 124 and Ewart, p. 152.
10. *Tutte le poesie* p. 60.
11. Vittorio Sereni, *Senza l'onore delle armi* (Milan, 1986) p. 55 and translated by Perryman and Robinson in *Numbers* I.1, Autumn 1986, p. 82.
12. Giovanni Raboni, in *Poesia italiana: il Novecento*, vol. 2 ed. Gelli and Lagorio (Milan, 1980) p. 643.
13. Fortini, *L'ospite ingrato*, 2nd edn. (Casale Monferrato, 1985) p. 16.
14. For Sereni's response, see *Tutte le poesie* p. 237.
15. Leonardo Sciascia in an interview cited by Marco Forti on the cover of *Diario d'Algeria* (Milan, 1965).
16. Fortini, *Saggi italiani* 1 p. 192 and Ewart, p. 154.
17. Giorgio Caproni, 'Le risposte di Vittorio Sereni', in *La Poesia di Vittorio Sereni*, Atti del Convegno (Milan, 1985) p. 14.
18. Vittorio Sereni cited in Umberto Saba, *Tutte le poesie* edited by Arrigo Stara (Milan, 1988) p. lxxxix.
19. Vittorio Sereni, *Gli immediati dintorni*, 2nd edn. (Milan, 1983) p. 65.
20. See Grillandi, op. cit. p. 55.
21. 'A Letter from Vittorio Sereni' in *PN Review* 5 (1977) p. 42.
22. *Gli immediati dintorni* p. 130.
23. *Tutte le poesie* p. 197.
24. Dego, op. cit. p. 31.

25. Montale, op. cit. p. 331 and Singh, p. 94.
26. Dego, op. cit. p. 31.
27. *Senza l'onore delle armi*, pp. 59–60 and *Numbers*, pp. 86–7.
28. Ibid. p. 63 and *Numbers* p. 90.
29. *Tutte le poesie* p. 525.
30. Grillandi, op. cit. p. 3.
31. Ferdinando Camon, *Il Mestiere di poeta* (Milan, 1982) p. 127.
32. Maurizio Cucchi, 'Poeta, scaccia da me la memoria', in *Rinascita* no. 32, 27 August 1982, p. 23 and translated by Perryman and Robinson in *The Many Review* no. 2, Spring 1984, p. 5.
33. *Gli immediati dintorni* p. 132.
34. Franco Fortini, *Nuovi saggi italiani* 2 (Milan, 1987) p. 169.
35. *Tutte le poesie* p. 290.
36. Ibid. p. 287. The lines from Poe's poem which Sereni quotes are 'Lo! 'tis a gala night / Within the lonesome latter years!' in *The Poems of Edgar Allan Poe*, ed. Mabbott (Cambridge Mass., 1980) p. 325, translated as 'Ecco si spiega una notturna danza / in cuore ai solitari ultimi anni.'
37. See, for example, *Tutte le poesie* pp. 134–5.

FROM

Frontier

(1941)

BIRTHDAY

Another bridge
beneath my feet, you lead me
where, ponderous city,
from flags and heights of houses
your breath hangs.
Again I hear
the birdsong merging
distant into sleep
and, bitter summer,
you renew me the time
of the pallid green, return
me the memory of a woman
whose looks are serene.

But where you open
and amid grasses, cart-tracks
and squares and streets disperse in dust,
you evoke me an image of water
and a calm of smiling windows.
Leaves' timeliness, lake's curve
you unfold me another age gleaming,
in a windless road extend
youth that finds no release.

[1936]

FOG

Here the traffic wavers
held up at the light
of the still signals.
I come to a place
where the city condenses
and a breath from blast furnaces spirits it away.
I ask the heart for a voice, above me looms
a persistent clamour
of distant factories, of forges.

And the weather tends towards winter.
I tramp the streets
which autumn adorned with green felts
in the days of delicate foxes,
the avenues sky-blue after rain.
At the light's sign the way is made free
and over these lands the year lingers.

At a turning, an ephemeral sun,
a cluster of mimosa
flares within the whitest fog.

[1937]

STORM AT SALSOMAGGIORE

Tonight you are close and threatening.
From the plain cities flare
in the last hour of convoys and the enemy
wind presses at the gates,
engulfs the squares and mists the globes
of the elegant street.
                    Along roads
your grace and the memory
of dazzling parasols dims
under warm, golden clouds.

Nor will it come back
in tranquil hours of sleep,
the muffled tapping of the wells
which measured nights. The passers-by
all have a face of death,
Emilia, on avenues
where leaves are frenzied.
The weather dies away and you also are dead.

You grasp me again in the gardens' air.
Dripping jasmine are reopening
to soothe the night, the town is populated
once more at a theatre's exit.
Your face is returning,
you want to punish the sullen fantasies.

In the rumble that grows distant
of final thunderclaps flying over houses,
I smile at your people
under resonant roofs, listening.

[1938]

TO M.L. PASSING ABOVE HER TOWN
IN AN EXPRESS TRAIN

Be untroubled by the roar
which bursts with me into your peaceful morning
if I lean out a little to recognize you,
while you perhaps are walking
with your people
across the beaming lands;
be untroubled by this fretfulness which touches you
and behind itself leaves a brief wind
of motes in a swirl of sounds.

How you brighten,
how you consent to the fugitive love
from the balconies, from gardens, from towers
. . . .

[1938–40]

DIANA

Your sky of those days returns
above the Lombard lofts,
thickens in clouds of heat
and every blue an exile in your eyes,
gathers and reposes.

Also the freshening hour will come
with the wind which lifts on the wharves
of the Navigli and the sky
that grows distant along their banks.

Diana, do you also return
amid tables paraded in the open
and people intent on their drinks
under the faraway moon?

A muted orchestra hums;
on the air which jerks from it here
I recognize your swaying walk,
the proud name sweetens in the evening
should somebody murmur it
across your wake.

June comes quickly
and the parched flower of sleep
grown in the saddest suburbs

and the song you had in the evening
returns to ache within here,
breathes on the memory
to reprove you my dying.

[1938]

SOLDIERS IN URBINO

These towers high in the memory
when the ramparts are at peace
and the fog is barely
drawing autumn onto these lands,
onto us
two, wandering soldiers. You say,
– *unhappily* – and choke back
a name if a leaf torn from who knows
where brushes against you,
then you speak of a star
which one day once more
over your path will perhaps appear.

Perhaps only from today
will we feel the hours' surge
curving halfway through our century,
even as the wind rocks the lamps
a portico whispers in shadow
and you start at the rumble
of lorries gnawing the mountain.

[1939]

3 DECEMBER

At the final tumult of the lines
peace comes to you, where the city
in a flight of bridges and avenues
hurls itself into the country
and those who pass don't know
about you just as you don't know
about the echoes of the hunts touching you.

Peace perhaps is truly yours
and the eyes we closed
for ever now reopened
are astonished
that still for us
you die a little every year
on this particular day.

[1940]

TO YOUTH

It's begun, a raucous song
of frogs among the hills
and from a mortal summer
– perhaps the last for you –
swallows hurl themselves headlong
in flight, like you walking
towards an unfathomable, foggy air.

And, of the voices straying
far from me, which one
will be able to turn your journey and mine
towards a march of sleepless sunflowers?
But no other good or other evil do they know
than a lake of blue or grey,
your eyes from an avenue's shadow.

[1941]

WINTER IN LUINO

You stretch out and breathe in the colours.
Along the restless bay,
in coal-heaps jagged in the sun
the outskirts of the town
glitter and abandon themselves.
I gather your heart
if in deep silence I'm moved
by a murmur of people through the streets.
Dead in foggy dusks of other skies
I survive your celestial evenings,
the occasional late boats
speckled with lights.
When you tend towards sleep
and sound with clogs and singing
and I'm lingering bewildered at your crossroads
you kindle for me in the dark of a square
a light of calm, a window pane.
I'll flee when the wind
sweeps your shores;
the harbour people know how vain
is the limpid days' defence.
At night the town is searched by rays,
sleepless fires edge round it
straying in the countryside,
a faint rumble of distant
locomotives towards the frontier.

[1937]

TERRACE

Suddenly the evening seizes us.
                                     You no longer know
whereabouts the lake finishes;
only a murmur
skims over our life
beneath a suspended terrace.

We're all hanging
on a mute event this evening
in that torpedo-boat's searchlight
which scrutinizes us then turning vanishes.

[1938]

ZENNA ROAD

We will arise on the lakeside
to infinite crossings. But now
in listless summertime
death grows more remote.
Yet still with traceless steps
we're setting out over ashen fields
through streets that border Elysium.

It alters,
the incalculable smile
is a scowl stretched between water
and shores in a wailing
of wind through the tinkling fencework.
The silence has this cadence,
dumbfounded to a cloud of smoke
left behind here from the surge
which just now divided the frontier.

You see on the deserted beach
the sand's whirling,
days' ashes overwhelm us.
And all around is the extended torment
of the sirens' farewells in the ports
for whoever remains in dreams
of fierce pallid faces,
in the rumble of the cloudburst
that thrashes the houses.
But we'll return silent at each approach to shore,
be no more than a sound,
you and I, of voluble hours
or perhaps short thuds of oars
from disconsolate boats.

You the dead never give us any peace
and it may be the wail
that goes through the leaves is yours
in the hour that the Lord clouds over.

[1938]

SEPTEMBER

Already in the gardens the fragrant olea
stings us with bitterness: the lake withdraws
from us somewhat, reveals a beach
of dried-up things,
of shattered oars, of shredded nets.
And the wind that brightens the vineyards
is already turning into firm days these lands
from a doubtful swarming summer.

In already certain death
we will walk with more courage,
slowly forward with the dogs we'll wade
into the tiny rolling wave.

[1938–40]

YOUR MEMORY IN ME

Your memory in me is a solitary
whirring of pedal-bikes that go
peaceably where the height
of noon descends
to the more blazing sunset
amongst gates and houses
and wistful inclines
of windows reopened onto summer.
What's left of me, only
a faraway wail of steam-trains lingers,
of souls that are departing.

And light on the wind there you leave,
lose yourself in the evening.

[1938–40]

CREVA ROAD

I

Soon May's freshest sail
will return across the waters
where infinite Luino trembles
and far away the song will appear
of the cuckoo looking out towards valleys
after the most recent rain:
                                now
one mad winter in the Saints' days
devoted to the snows
lizards move through hedgerows,
all around the forests steam
and a couple lingering on slopes
have voices of greeting for me
as on the mountains sometimes
people calling to each other across valleys.

II

This timorous living amongst the dead.

But where this bluer, always bluer
sky opens out and leads us
to the furthest villages,
looking at them, every colour fades.
You know that if the road descends
to us it extends other fields, other villages,
other sails on the lakes:
                          again the wind
disturbs the bays, obscures them.
We go back a step into winter.

And to the gloomy dwellings we go back,
at a banquet of enchanting guests
dying fires are rekindled.

And other days die in the glasses.

Then save us from the horrors of night,
the lights in silent houses.

[1941]

SEE HOW THE VOICES FALL

See how the voices fall and friends
are so far distant
that a cry is less
than a murmur to call them.
But upon the years is returning
your transparent fatal smile
similar to the lake
which carries off boats and men
but brings colour to our mornings.

[1940]

FROM
Algerian Diary
(1947)

OUTSKIRTS 1940

Youth is all in the light
of a city at sunset
where tormented and exiled every sound
stands out from the hum.

And my life save yourself if you can
spare yourself for who's to come
passing and those semblances on bridges
in the headlamps' glare.

CITY AT NIGHT

Restless in the troop train
which sweeps so slowly against you
I lean towards your ominous lights
in the sighing of the trees.

Meanwhile you sleep and perhaps
someone is dying in the upper rooms
and you roll away with a face
behind each window – you yourself
a face, a face only
closing forever.

BOLOGNESE DIARY

I don't know how always
a desperate murmur oppresses me
in your midday air
so diffused on the hills within sunlight
so crowded and smoke-filled down here.
And there is no flower of yours fails to express
for me the evil which quickly gnaws it,
and no music at windows advancing
that doesn't fall bitterly back onto summer.
In vain beneath San Luca every road
voluptuously eases, I am blind
and defenceless to your joy.
And gilded shadow brims in evening's pyre,
love grows brutal on the faces,
beyond townships the irreparable time
of our cowardice is fleeing.

BELGRADE

to Giosue Bonfanti

                – . . . Donau? –
– Nein Donau, Sava – as in a dream
the sentry says and a bridge
drums beneath the lingering convoy.
And I don't know what remote depth
of labour and voices from your parapets
celebrates a peaceful hour in Europe
born with you between two chimeras
– the Danube! the Sava! –
azure in a morning lost,
to come to pass:
unforeseen dream of memories, as
the sentries dream
from the bridges of the Sava
some figure among the trees at random,
a love romance just caught sight of.

Mestre–Athens troop train, August 1942

ITALIAN IN GREECE

First Athens evening, drawn-out goodbye
of the convoys that file off about your margins
brimming with misery in the long half-dark.
Like a grief
I've left summer on the curves
and sea and desert's my tomorrow
without more seasons.
Europe, Europe who watch me
descending unarmed and absorbed
in my slender myth amid the ranks of the brutal,
I'm one of your sons in flight who knows
no enemy if not his own sorrow
or some reawakened tenderness
of lakes, of fronds behind the steps
that are lost,
I'm clothed in sun and dust,
go to damn and bury myself in sand for years.

Piraeus, August 1942

DIMITRIOS

to my daughter

To the tent approaches
the little enemy,
Dimitrios, and takes me unawares,
tiny bird's cry
on the glass of midday sun.
The pure mouth's not twisted
by the grace which asks for bread,
not veiled in tears
the glance that hunger and fear
dissolves in childhood's sky.

He's already far,
sharp will-o'-the-wisp
who evaporates in heat-haze,
Dimitrios – on miserly lands
barely believable, barely
living tremor
of me, of my life
wavering on the ocean.

Piraeus, August 1942

THE ATHENIAN GIRL

Now the day's a sigh
and all of Attica a shade.
And as a flash illumines the opaque
windows turning in flight
so your face sparkles down there
from the circle of light you kindle
to the evening icon.
                    But here
where more and more scarce
the last hunt's prey falls to earth
among trees that follow the border,
alas the pure
sign of your syllables is rotten,
alters to twisted cyrillic.
And you: how little by little you darken.
See how you cannot remain, are lost
within the last viaduct's roar.

            *

Soon I'll be the bewildered traveller
hazarded out in foggy weather.

Weak flights, by now inert names
one by one notes fall away
to tear themselves from the chorus,
dark glimpses of a lost sojourn: Kaidari,
a bittersweet vale of olives
in my idle recalling – or those
boats perplexed in the wind of Piraeus.

And all that took the eye and ear
nailed into the mist is already passed.

*

Because the wheel has turned so much
a friendly fleet cruises offshore today,
anxiety's fruit is ripened late,
first harvest to others than you,
dcspinís.
Whoever sleeps sleeps in the high snows
up there among the dear dead ones.
With the dead you arise and in them speak:
– I want a banner
to resound with my torment
radiant with my lament,
I want a land where it is song
light from the green years,
the hymn which weighed upon me,
where the alarm that furrowed nights
returns changed to an echo
of hope, of mercy, of fear – .

*

So, distant, we converge.
And at times it seems
we step out, despinís, in sunlight
kindly also to the defeated
in the vivid gardens of Attica.

And still your memory grows verdant with them.

Athens–Mestre troop train, autumn 1942
North Africa, autumn 1944

ALGERIAN DIARY

to Remo Valianti

    1

Over there where from tower
to tower agreement
leaps in vain now and is thrown back,
the who-goes-there of the hour,
– just as down here from turret to turret
from the heights of the compound
Moroccan guards call to each other –
who goes in the gloomy midnight's
quick snowflakes, who misses
the final toast on the wind's
black thresholds, sinister
with waiting, who goes . . .
It's an image of ours
distorted, not come
to light, which abandons
a blue vein of oblivion only
between two eras dead within us.

Sainte-Barbe du Thélat, New Year's Day 1944

2

An unexpected vacancy of heart
among the camp beds of Sainte-Barbe.
The heartfelt faces fade, I remain alone
with a swirl of wearisome voices.

And the clearest voice is no more
than a pummelling of rain on the tents,
one final sonorous frond
on these marshes of sleep
coursed at times by a dream.

Sainte-Barbe du Thélat, winter 1944

3

Valour and grace
are born again.
No matter in what forms – a game
of football between prisoners:
                              specially in him
playing out on the wing.
O you so light and quick across fields
shadow that extends
in tenacious sunset.
It contorts, flames at length on the end
of a colourless day and as your run
is blurring chimerical now
grows great within me
bitter in the wake.

Sainte-Barbe du Thélat, May 1944

4

He knows nothing any more, is borne up on wings
the first fallen splayed on the Normandy beaches.
That's why someone tonight
touched my shoulder murmuring
pray for Europe
while the New Armada
drew on the coast of France.

I replied in my sleep: – it's the wind,
the wind which makes strange music.
But if you truly were
the first fallen splayed on the Normandy beaches,
you pray if you can, I am dead
to war and to peace.
This, the music now:
of the tents that flap against the poles.
It's not the music of angels, it's my own
music only and enough – .

Camp Hospital 127, June 1944

5

Alas how what returns
on the leafy mid-July
Algerian hillside
of you in the tall grass lain down
is the voice not ingenuous
nor even perverse
complaining of the heat
and the untamed mouth

but hoarse a little and tender only . . .

Saint-Cloud, July 1944

6

They don't know they're dead
the dead like us,
they have no peace.
Stubbornly they repeat life,
speak words of goodness to each other,
reread the age-old signs in the sky.
A grey circle runs in Algeria
through the months' derision
but the axis is fixed to a scorched name: ORAN.

Saint-Cloud, August 1944

7

Only the summer is true and this
its light which evens you out.
And may everyone discover
the evergreen tree, the cone of shade,
the blissful purifying water
and the spider's web woven with tedium
on the evil ponds
remain a vernicle of rainbows.
Down there, the frail hedgerow, a halo
of red powder,
but like the grave the German crowd's
song to their lost power.

Now every frond is silent
oblivion's shell compact
the circle perfect.

Saint-Cloud, August 1944

8

And again in a dream the tent's edge
is flapping.
Camp of a year ago
I drag myself back to
but no one any longer
suffers here on their knees
only earth suffers
that people no longer
suffer being here
and all's made ready for eternity
the brief lake become marshes
evil weeds grown to the thresholds
nor does accordion groan
lost Sundays
amongst fond gatherings
of the desperate less desperate
more desperate. I say:
– Where is the lamp
young Walter watched over
flaming in the small hours
to the wakeful company . . . –.

Sidi-Chami, October 1944

9

Often through tortuous alleys
quelque part en Algérie
of the indefinite place
that the wind gusts bite,
your rainfall your sunlight
all at one point
amongst bitter briars of the more
bitter iron wire, thorn with no rose . . .
but already a year's gone by,
it is barely a dream:
we're all subdued to remember.

A clear phantom laughs
where the sentry was
and the hillside
of our absent spirits
deserted, and beyond recall, veils over.

Sidi-Chami, November 1944

10

Too late the time has come
for you to be spoken
the pain of my young years.

The city grew pallid in the wind
or a rainbow fell into the dance
of graced reflections:
you were in the meditative ticking
of a dial at my wrist
among pages leafed over
a flooding of sunlight,
clear suburbs' idleness
quickly assumed on a face
scrutinized so deeply
but a glittering eye, but a feverish touch.

Faint shadows came: – what do you
bring, what offer? . . . – I smiled
at my friends, they vanished,
the curve of the avenue
vanished in sadness.
Behind wheels in flight
poppies over fields were
smothered in an ashen summer.

But if you're missing
and even the sky's defeated
I'm a stunted glimmer,
a superfluous voice in the choir.

Sidi-Chami, November 1944

11

If fever for you no more sustains me

how each gesture's changed to a caress
where a goodbye wavers,
leaf which in early summer's
torn away.

My gaze is made more tender and slow
no longer stretched to be elsewhere and here.

Streets fountains squares
flown through one day
in the lamp of your body
at each I linger in a tangle
of loved faces
in the little green between dark passages
beneath the old sky grown mild.

Sidi-Chami, December 1944

12

In the smuggled glass
it soon reaches the dregs
this gaiety veiling sadness
in the plume of quenched brands
hurled to us from the most distant fire.
And be the God made flesh today
distance for us in the darkest hour.

Sidi-Chami, Christmas 1944

THE AFRICAN SICKNESS

to Giansiro going to Algeria (1958)

A lone motorcycle.
In tunnels, along miserable
elevated sections of Milan,
a soul delayed. What of it?
It's gone, and makes its way now
and an echo barely returns to us,
with the family pot's bubbling
in these times which quieten down.
Different from Oran,
the train's roll sang at the war's end
and what fine sun on the journey and swarms
of little black kids, darker and darker,
station after station,
already with all Algeria behind us.
To think – I said – the war is ending
and west-south-west,
what a roundabout way to send us home.
And from the black kids, darker and darker,
station after station,
give me bonbon good American please,
the beseeching litany. Between viaducts
and bridges the echo rebounded
through a February of untimely flowers,
returned to spitting stewpots
steaming gaily in the sun
and to that feverish, then ever fainter
rhythm of Ramadan
persisting day after day in our ears,
we halted and there,
chalked within the verb
to hope, the verb to desire,

was Casablanca.
                    And then?
I saw men with twisted
limbs – O bidonville! –
baracans swell in the gale,
other petals flare – *'they're perennial asters,*
no, flowers doomed to die', the speeches
of captivity –
turn to summer dust,
and when we'd stopped expecting it almost
we were on resounding swell,
heading for a holiday
of faces over there beyond the sea,
from a blackish distance, in the family
with seagulls that trustful
gave themselves up to the wave.
But every breeze dropped, past
Morocco sailing for the isle of Sards
a fever grew in me:
no longer that maddening
rhythm of Ramadan
                    but an eagerness,
a fretting to arrive
the more so on evenings
of stagnant low water
when the wave darkened,
broken by feeble glimmers – and
                    Gibraltar! a howl,
the raised snout of Europe,
from the bitch crouched there on front paws:
Late, too late for the feast
– the foul throat taunted –
too late! and something else more confused
about the badly understood
verb of white Casablanca.

*

This burbling, pursuit or escape I don't know,
now ten or more years old
about one journey among many . . . – your eyes grow
    troubled –
and no news of Algeria.
No, none – I reply. Or barely some convulsive
chokings of memory: a day never ended,
always at sunset – and barefoot, in rags
on the back of a donkey, but with the helmet
of Africa on his head still,
a prisoner like me
quickly out of sight behind the hill.
What was left of the empire . . .
                            and the penny whistle
roaming between tents to stave off boredom
and, no sooner silent, that empty clearing
where the fire went past and the gypsies . . .
Wounds of the world you bear
and recount them in Milan
among blue windows of a sunny winter
at Christmas, while – *Symphonie* in houses,
through foggy streets *Symphonie d'amour* – the younger
generation striving to revive the dance.

It's us, don't you realize, we're the younger
generation – you almost shout in my face –
with at least ten years owed us on the civil register . . .

Bring me news of Algeria
– I almost shout in return – of what
of us passed outside the barbed wire,
tell me they weren't only
ghosts pressed from the heat-haze,
of us ever late for the war

but ever on the outskirts
of a real war of our own . . . if what
our fever of that time was spreading
is only slaughter, torture, isolation,
or a people that religiously kill.

This is what I had to say,
this tangle to unravel
in the final spasm of youth,
this toad to spit out,
but to you good luck and *bon voyage*,
the family pot's bubbling, bubbling.

SEPTEMBER THE EIGHTH

'43/'63

Sale macaroni rains on the memory
the refrain's clamour taunting

but disembodied, flown from its sense

such as for a whole afternoon
could perhaps drain away
live as rhythm as pillow-talk
inside an Oran room over the tangle
of a panting couple, of a copula
negro-french
franco-american
occupied with something quite other
– us others in rags outside there on the wharves and

sale macaroni the rain
sale macaroni the leaves
sale macaroni the ships in the harbour
sale macaroni de mon amour
the war rolled on elsewhere.

FROM
The Human Implements
(1965)

VIA SCARLATTI

With you and no other
is the word.

Between two gulfs of cries, not long,
the street, all houses, runs;
but suddenly a breach opens it
where gaunt kids break through
and the sun perhaps in spring.
Now, within, it seems always evening.
Beyond, it grows still darker,
the street is ashes and smoke.
But the faces, the faces I can't say:
shadow on shadow of exhaustion and rage.
Clicking heels of teenagers
mock at that pain,
the improvised strain of an opera duet
at a small crowd converging.

And here for you I wait.

JOURNEY THERE AND BACK

I'll go back down the way we came
a while ago
when never more beautiful the moon startled you.
There remains to me a city close to sleep
in earliest springtime.
O fire that now you are
fading, O confused ashes
of countryside which darkens and smoulders,
O screech that crumbles the air
and with it splits my heart in two.

THE MISAPPREHENSION

From beyond a twittering barrier of children
she seemed both to cry and smile at me.
But whatever was she wanting with her look,
the blonde and mournful passer-by?
Between us was my returning look
and, audible barely, a voice:
love – it was singing – *and beauty reborn*...
So, straying, the voice affirmed
and lost itself upon those
bitter and sweet spring avenues.
It was the gradual glimmer we sometimes
saw lap the faces' margins
and, barely kindled, in weakness shrink away.

ON THE ZENNA ROAD AGAIN

Why do these troubled branches touch me?
Maybe because they repeat the green's renewed
each spring, but joy doesn't flourish afresh?
But this time it's not my lament
and it's not spring, it's summer,
the summer of my years.
Under my eyes brought on by the road
the coastline is forming itself
always unchanged and not changed by my roar
nor, lower, that sudden wind which troubles it
and at the next bend will, perhaps, die down.
And I'll be able to despair for what changes,
carry round a burning head of sorrow . . .
but the obscure threading of the things
I suppose back there: the pulley in the well,
the wheels of cable-ways through woods,
the least acts, the poor
human implements bound to the chain
of necessity, the fishing line
cast for nothing through centuries,
the meagre lives which for the eye of one returning
who finds nothing, not a thing has really altered
repeat themselves identically,
those flurrying arms that will soon fall back,
those hands pointlessly fresh
which stretch towards me and the privilege
of motion reproach me . . .
So pity then for the troubled branches
called forth a moment in the spiral of wind
which will soon drop away from me
waving goodbye goodbye.

And now already changed the roar
checks an instant and then is released
out of immense sleep
and another landscape turns and goes by.

WINDOW

Suddenly – you notice – it's come,
the spring's come suddenly
we were waiting years for.

I watch you offered to that green
to the living breath to the wind,
to what other I don't know and fear
– and stay in hiding –
and were my heart touched I would die.
But I know too well if I lean
out on the avenue's cry,
I'm too unlike that green
which on the balconies moves a living breath,
from the incredible cricket that this year
appears at dusk amongst roofs of the city
– and closed in me I stay, sealed in disgust.

And yet, a day was enough.
How many clouds for one that came
have set themselves in motion
that closer run closer over the green,
smother song and tomorrow
and want our sky menacing.
Tell me then if you still know
I'm your song forever,
the living breath, your own
perennial green, the voice which loved and sang –
which competing now, you listen to?,
over roofs it flushes out that bit of spring
and searches and strains and resigns itself again.

THE SHARKS

What escapes of us on the line of the current?
Oh, of a story that didn't have a sequel
shreds of sun, wan faces, random
fishing lamps a moment revives
and the holed straw hat
this last summer abandons to us.
Our summers, you see,
memory you still have desires:
in you the bow is drawn from the seafront
but the point flies to my heart no more.
Half-asleep you hear the sea's
smooth vigil and behind it
certain festive voices.

And soon frustrated by the prey
down there sharks furrowing the gulf
soon they'll rip each other to pieces.

YEARS AFTER

The splendid the delirious rain has eased,
kisses us with rare final droplets.
Outside again
love is close by me and friendship.
And that murmur, until just then almost imploring,
from the darkened portico
rumbles at my back now, breaks from my past:
faces unaltered they'll be, same as ever,
with an old air congealed in them today.
Even our own, amongst those, of that time?
Then do not turn away love I beg you
and friendship remain and defend us.

SIX IN THE MORNING

Death breaks the seal, just so, of everything.
And in fact, I came back,
the door wasn't properly shut
the panel barely ajar.
And in fact I'd been dead a short while,
done for in not many hours.
But what I saw, plainly,
the dead don't see:
visited by my recent death, the house
only barely disturbed
still warm with me who no longer existed,
the bar snapped,
purposeless the bolt
and a great and peopled atmosphere
about me, little in death,
one after another the avenues
of Milan awakened in all that wind.

DISCOVERY OF HATRED

Here was the wrong, here the inveterate error:
to believe that nothing could be gained but love.
Oh the packs of cheerful masks
oh the music-making parties in polite districts . . .
The highest balcony gives back other music
to the night and beyond city gates
the road stretches blossoming once more?
Then come, late on, come a time
of real fire between you and me,
let the righteous fight flare up at last,
you masks, and your subtle games
of disfigured love: in exactly
my way of unowed and dissipated
love, you people, I'll put you to the flames.

THOSE CHILDREN PLAYING

will one day forgive
if we soon get out of the way.
They'll forgive. One day.
But the time's twistedness,
life's course deviated down false tracks,
the haemorrhage of days
from the pass of corrupted awareness:
this, no, they won't forgive.
You don't forgive a woman for deceitful love,
the smiling land of water and leaves
that's torn apart revealing
putrefied roots, black slime.
'*In love there are no sins*',
raged a poet in his final years,
'*there are only sins against love.*'
And these, no, they will not forgive.

SABA

Beret pipe stick, the lifeless
objects of a memory.
But I saw them brought to life on one
roaming in an Italy of dust and rubble.
Always he talked of himself
but like no one I've known who talking of themselves
and demanding life of others in his talk
gave as much and so much more
to anyone who'd stay and listen.
And one day, a day or two after the 18th of April,
I saw him wandering from square to square
from one Milan café to another
hounded by the radio.
'Bitch' – he was railing – 'bitch.' In amazement
people looked at him.
It was Italy he meant. Abrupt, as to a woman
who knowingly or not has wounded us to death.

PASSING

A single day, not that. An hour or two.
Light you never see.
Flowers you'd not dream of for an August.
On the fields spots of blood,
towards the sea no oleanders yet.
Hot, but no real wish to go swimming.
Wafted Tyrrhenian Sunday.
Am I already dead and come back here?
Or the only one living in the vivid and still
nothing of a memory?

SITUATION

The force of the commonplace,
grievous.
The sprinkler jet in the grasses,
unnoticed sigh.
The garden as evening draws in.
Chairs, in a circle, reclining.
Familiar glances cross: one only evasive.
For the most part calm.

On the reverse of the commonplace,
the vespers bells. Unheeded.
For century after century at this hour
a still warm coil
of blood and sense.
And round about the swallows in their thousands.

I am all of this, the common
place and its reverse
beneath the vault as the last light withdraws.
But nothing can this do against a single
glance of others, self-assured, taking flame
from my own glance
against your guilty eyes,
against the furtive steps that are bearing you away.

THE FRIENDS

You remember them in '51
Giuliana and Giancarlo
dancers and tumblers as they were
with a calling for poverty
whose like would inherit the earth tomorrow,
health youth spirit zest.
And now? On a dull
morning in '60? With them and their lovely
and terrible children
whose calling for poverty's intact,
their like may still inherit the earth
tomorrow,
isn't the mouth of the Magra
for the tenth summer adorned afresh?
What times – you murmur – always more muddled
what turmoil of boats and engines
what an assortment of fauna on the sea.
Don't leave me alone here
                            – you're about
to cry – come back . . .
But there from behind a rock
always strong on the oars
to the rescue Giancarlo appears.

And to you it seems a miracle.

APPOINTMENT AT AN UNUSUAL HOUR

The city – I tell myself – where shade
is almost more delightful than sunshine,
how it sparkles all new in the morning . . .
' . . . dries out last night's storm' – my own
joy laughs, returned beside me
after a brief separation.
'Dries out its contradictions in the sun'
– grim, near giving in already, I retort.
But the form, the picture, semblance
– an angel's I'd have said in other times –
reborn beside me in the window-pane:
'Dear' – she openly teases me – 'dear,
with that holiday face of yours. And thinking
of the socialist city?'
She's won. And already I'm melting: 'No,
I won't get to see it,' I reply.
       (We'll no longer
be together, I should say.) 'But it's right,
you do well to ignore me if I say these things,
say them from hatred of someone
or anger at something. But believe in the other
which from time to time takes hold in me,
includes all others in itself, gives them splendour,
rare as this September morning . . .
I was speaking to myself about just you:
about joy.'
    She takes me by the arm.
'No, it isn't rare,' – I correct myself – 'it exists,
you bear it like a wound
through the dazzling streets. It's this
moment in September repressed in me all year,
it's the stolen fox the boy
hid beneath his clothes and it tore his thigh,

a weapon you carry without license, beyond
the brief dream of a holiday.
                                         I could
kill with this, with joy alone . . .'

But where are you, wherever have you gone?

'This is what I think of should someone
speak to me of revolution,'
I say to the window-pane empty once more.

IN SLEEP

I

Late, you too have heard them –
those steps that climbed towards death
squadded together
from a September's scattered ranks
from its golds already chill, to re-enter the closed,
compulsory ranks of how many pre-militarized Sundays
reinventing them with all the force
of the pride and scorn of the feet, the bashfulness
of history's confirmation candidates,
over earthworks, through firing ranges,
extras in the footlights that then go into the dark
– and plenty of strength still to dash through gunfire,
to smash down walls, fly over years,
those steps of theirs reached to you.

II

All through the city, in the streets
for a while still deserted an assiduous scraping,
manifestos in pieces, the promises of yesterday
in shreds and along the pavements
already the remains of sliced cicadas.
Climbed down at the crossing, a tramdriver
operates the points with his bar,
restarts the days and noise.
– These the only losers, the real defeated ... –
an anonymous voice admonishes.

III

Abruptly the arm is forced down
and the winner's hand passes
to others, more powerful.
I'll declare it was just
and attempt a composure
barely contradicted by the maddened eyes.
That will soon be lifeless.
On dignity's shirt-collar
soon dishonour's caterpillar . . .

IV

Will the half-wit take the bait
of the boys in the bar?
Obviously he'll bite
                    and for a nothing,
in his fogginess he'll find
he's on the wrong side.
They'll beat him, after, with all the more relish.
Was there ever anything else to do on Sundays?
Newspapers round the kiosks
garrulous in the spring wind:
up comes this man, vermin in fine linen,
sets his hound on the headlines and pictures.
– Filthy politics
and us always ready to settle the damages,
Pantalones that pay –
and tosses coins to the scurrying newsagent.
Around: approvals, laughter.

V

Italy, one endless Sunday.
Scooters bring the summer,
the dejection of the feast's end.
Vainly the last ball, a while back, flashed by
and it's lost: but already
the winning cycle wheel's glittering.
And after, what to do on Sundays?
Goad the dog, incite the madman . . .
I don't like my times, I don't like them.
Italy will slumber with me.
In a Lombard or Emilian garden
there's always one like me
with suspicions and thoughts of guilt
between a nightingale's song
and espalier of roses . . .

VI

or else
a couple between quarries and meadows.
Development area – quite soon
we'll reach here with the houses.
And meantime while it lasts
let's abandon ourselves to these false fields.
      Where are you lost love
the man sings to the girl
who's skipped beyond the embankment.
'The sun always shines on yours' blue-eyes
continues to tease her, finding her once more
over there, the wind-blown hair, young throat,
even blonder in that returning sun.
But then, divided by the crowd
walking apart *among the crowd that doesn't know*,

what survives of a day? of us or us two?
    The parting, the going away
on the line of a tune in another time already
    looking into each face
        and it's not you.
Then is youth ended here,
in a mistaken identity?
Of course, that file of roofs
those balconies and terraces
quick link between us each morning
and slow flight every evening . . .
already tomorrow you could give yourself up to
another wave of traffic, attempt
a different slope,
change company and district
       and leave me
on one of these downfalls of the heart, these sudden
clearings in the city
with a loss's bitterness
with those late heard steps of theirs.
Solitude, only pride . . .
      From them
to us a hidden wound groans
and the wind from the plains gives it voice,
petrifies it on the headstones.

THE LINES

They're being written still.
You think of them lying
to anxious eyes that wish you well
the last evening of the year.
They're written in the negative
within a blackness of years
like paying a tiresome
debt that goes back years.
No, the task's no longer happy.
Some laugh: you were writing for Art.
Not even I wanted that, I wanted something else.
Lines are made to shrug off a burden
and move on to the next one. But there's always
one burden too many, there's never
any line that's enough
if tomorrow you yourself forget it.

THE ALIBI AND THE BENEFIT

The doors flung open for nothing onto evening fog
no one who gets on or off but
a gust of smog the newsboy's cry
– paradoxical – il Tempo di Milano the alibi
and the benefit of fog things hidden
proceed under cover move towards me
veer away from me gone past like history gone past
like remembrance: the twenty the thirteen the
    thirty-three
years like tramcars' numerals
or sole winking clue of the lost root
a foggy evening at the intersections of all possible
    evenings
in fact *it's any evening crossed by half-empty trams*
you see me advance as you know in districts without memory
never seen a district quite so rich in memories
as these claimed to be 'without' in the young Erba's lines
between two thick barriers inside an acrid grey tunnel
how painfully the transport pierces fog this evening
alibi but benefit of the fog all possible worlds
that hide themselves only to blossom
in trees and fountains this dust of years of Milan.

POETRY IS A PASSION?

The embrace which repels and doesn't unite –
firm chin planted on that shoulder
of hers, the fixed and surly gaze:
others' story and, already old, their own.
He was dying of apprehension and jealousy
so much so he wished himself dead, he wished it
truly, there in her arms.
Angrily, he'd no wish to break free.
Who'll give in first? A Sunday
in August, outside, was at its height
and all of Italy in piazzas, bars,
on the avenues, stuck in front of televisions . . .
The slightest move, – he told himself – try to be a man
and you'll escape the bewitched circle.
And, the convulsive grip persisting
(which on instinct she redoubled),
blindly one hand fumbled with the set,
turned a dial: in the room
at once the race appeared, and came between them.

The champion they say is finished,
who seemed immune to time's derision
and from minute signs, season after season,
they say he just can't make it, but instead
in the race that for him is to the death
he still makes it, he's his champion.
They were waiting for him in the final stretch:
'if we see a certain
jersey appear down there . . .' and something announces
    it,
a shuffle of people down on the corner,
a rustle of voices which approaches,
a clamouring, a roar, it's incredible, it's him,

he's on his own, he's sat up, raised his hands,
he has made it . . . and so I too
can rally, beat them hollow.
The eyes meanwhile had softened
and, loosening a little, the grip
grew tender, acquired another sense, returned
with different violence.
For a voice irrupted into the room . . .
The instinct, which never fails her,
strikes always at just the right moment
amongst her simple thoughts.
She can understand her man: knows well
the more he imagines he beats them
the better she enthrals him
and holds him as long as she wants.
'Dearest' – she whispers in his ear – 'my love . . .'.
And the clear Sunday's still in the sky,
the avenue thick with greenery and birds,
houses and skyscrapers not yet ghostly,
just a little sharper at this hour
late in the afternoon, the final Sunday
of this our summer. And if it seems to him
a barely perceptible shudder encroaches
onto the still warm breeze that reaches
to the terrace: *August too*
– *she suddenly says, remembering* –
August too has gone for ever . . .

Yes I too have loved those lines . . .
too much even for my own liking.
But it was the only book come from
anyone's baggage. They wanted me to read them.
For three or four
evenings consecutively, going south
down the Drina's bottle-green to dazzling

Larissa, the Balkan troop train. Those lines
felt far away to me,
very far away from us: but it was what remained,
a manner of speaking between us –
smiling or foreboding, trusting or alarmed,
believing in the war or not believing –
during that summer of iron.   1942
Perhaps no one has caught so well
this moment in the year. Yet still
– and he looked around among the darkening roofs
and the first snaking lights of the city –
even they've gone *over there across serene rivers*,   d' Annunzio
it's not the same, another August,
doesn't touch those trees and roofs,
lives and dies and mourns itself
but elsewhere, but very very far from here.

. . . .

A DREAM

I was crossing the bridge
over a river that could have been the Magra
where I go for the summer, or even the Tresa,
in my part of the country between Germignaga and
    Luino.
A leaden body without face blocked my way.
'Papers,' he ordered. 'What papers,' I answered.
'Out with them,' he insisted, firm,
on seeing me look aghast. I made to appease him:
'I've prospects, a place awaiting me,
certain memories, friends still alive,
a few dead honourably buried.'
'Fairy tales,' – he said – 'you can't pass
without a programme.' And sneering he weighed
the few papers, my worldly goods.
I wanted one last try. 'I'll pay
on my way back if you'll let me
pass, if you'll let me work.'
We would never see eye to eye: 'Have you made'
– he was snarling – 'your ideological choice?'
Grappling we struggled on the bridge's parapet
in utter solitude. The fight
still goes on, to my dishonour.
I don't know
who'll end up in the river.

ON THE CREVA ROAD AGAIN

It could have been her, my grandmother
dead I don't know how many years.
Come out at late vespers
from her Catholic twilight,
at the time that's called St Martin's summer
or commemoration day.
An old woman scarlet with laughter.
The birds sang from the waterways
and how many still green leaves intact
autumn bore in her womb.
As we asked her the way
she was merry there before us
in the silk of her parasol,
in her outfit's sequins. And nothing
beside her scarlet laughter
was the Catholic twilight, nothing
her mourning weeds. And nor
do I know how much she saw of us
glowing from the day and whatever.
Perhaps in place of us she saw
a cloud and spoke to that:
'Fond disguise,' – she said – 'I know you,
so good at hiding in enchanting vapour.
I beheld you once before
on the still whole cheek of one
who for love, in search of
quiet waters, took her life:
with what resolve, what strength those hands
tendered to sleep weeds torn
from the final river margin.
I realize now, I didn't grieve at your end,
but for the strength which belied you

abandoning itself in you . . . Disguise called love,
fine thing you are!
                        For a little shade that makes
the waters quicker, bushes more fervent, June more lively
how many years of nothing after,
years of nave and hospital ward
of memory-dulling bells
of soot-filled dusks: until just now
there was such fine sun – and from idleness or boredom
or distraction we didn't walk out to enjoy it.
See how you've sullied my life
with humility and trembling.'

So railing about a lost strength,
a distant gladness, growing so faint beyond us
she uncovered, disgracing it, death
still hidden within us. And from that day
and that hour
my love I never spoke to you of love.

ON A CEMETERY PHOTOGRAPH

The witless smile that halted me between tombstones
and crosses, in the little forest
of the innocent dead, of lives
barely kindled and snuffed out in the whiteness
was my same astonishment
that over years he'd come so little way.

O slumberer, what kind of thing is sleep?
                              Sleep . . .

And here he is amongst the innocent babes
astonished in the marble
as if a Thou should truly
come again
to free the quick and dead.
And how much seed, what tears vainly shed.

TO A CHILDHOOD COMPANION

I

Not much is left to be said
and the same landscape's always repeated.
Nothing remains but to move round it,
we two in the wind bellowing pointless confidences
and taking them for recapitulations, striking
profundities on life.
                              'But you've the beauty....'.
                                          'Claptrap
in the shadowy wind, religion
of death: the years that pass
all the same, the hill that in autumn blazes again,
the campanili
flooded in sunlight undaunted,
petrified bones of the dead, our own
roots too similar, for too long
not to grieve together, which the wind
makes groan...'.

Soon an autostrada will bear a different wind
through these rapturous place-names: Creva,
Germignaga, Voldomino, la
Trebedora – they'll live again
with different sound and sense
in a light of self-esteem...
Not that this is beauty,
                    but
the final furlong whip, the peremptory
touch at affliction
that ruinously tosses within us,
knowing it's always one step beyond,
beauty, in a sparkling air:

this,
which the libertines darkly search for
and that work has taught me.

    II

Goodbye, goodbye the branches repeat.
Goodbye I too must say to you now
with the same tenderness
and intensity, the same
humility as the branches
which will continue rustling even so
beyond the immediate glance.
There's no one, it seems, on the bridge
that I'll recross in a while: no masked villain
of non-existence, no plaintive traveller.
It's clear up ahead then, stop having visions!
On the troubled Sunday
of a river at its mouth they come to grips
for my own good in me . . .

FROM HOLLAND

Amsterdam

Chance led me there between
nine and ten one Sunday morning,
turning at a bridge, one of many, to the right
along a canal half iced over. And not
this is the house, but merely
– seen a thousand times before –
'Anne Frank's house', on the simple plaque.

Later my companion said:
Anne Frank's shouldn't be, it isn't
a privileged memory. There were many
were broken simply out of hunger
without the time to write.
She, it's true, did write it.
But at every turn, at every bridge, along every canal
I continued to search for her, no longer finding her,
finding her perpetually.
That's why it's one and unfathomable Amsterdam
in its three or four varying elements
which it blends in many recurring wholes,
its three or four rotten or unripe colours
which its space perpetuates far as it stretches,
spirit that irradiates steadfast and clear
on thousands of other faces, everywhere
seed and bud of Anne Frank.
That's why Amsterdam's vertiginous on its canals.

The Interpreter

'Now they're returning. Florid, rowdy
loaded with currency.
They are good clients, can't be turned away.
Information, as much as they want.
Not a word more. It isn't a question
of grudges or retaliation.
But of unflinching memory.'

Volendam

Water here a hundred years back
– repeated Federico the guide –
today *polder*.
           Life
between *polder* and dyke, there's room here
for procreation only
and defence against death.
That's what the faces reddened by the cold say
outside the Catholic mass
at Volendam, the dirge
of the varying wind between sea-walls.
Love is for later, it's for the children
and it is greater. Take heed.

THE WALL

I am
almost in a dream in Luino
along the wall of the dead.
Here our faces glowed in the shade,
in the rosy light the trees rained
near nine of an evening in June?
Whoever dies of course ... but these the living
on the other hand: play nightly,
six a side, the younger generation
of Porto or the Verbanesi.
Turned from them, I sense
the animation of the leaves
and in that the storm making headway.
They cast dust and leafage, cast anger
those on the wall's far side –
and among them the most dear.
                                        'Papa' – in childish
self-defence – 'papa ...'

I've not much to resist him, the pang
of love, the start in me when I read
of flowerings in the winter's depths
on upland surrounding him in frost down there,
if I bring him news of his things
if I feel them worm-eaten (the two-faced
insidious fidelity of things:
able to outlast a man's life
and then crumble astonishing us years or moments after)
upon some shelf
in 27 Via Scarlatti, Milan.

He says it's self-interested love, foreseeing
I'll soon be frozen, tells me as if in glory

reassuring himself, reassuring me
while I reopen my eyes and he draws away laughing
– and those spirited lads still fooling against the storm
    and night –
with dust and leaves the length of the wall he says
that a summer's evening is a summer's evening
and there will be more sense now
to the song of the drunks around Creva.

THE BEACH

They've all gone away –
the voice was blathering down the receiver.
Then, knowingly: – They'll never return – .

But today
on this stretch of beach not visited before
those patches of sunlight ... Signals
of them, who hadn't left at all?
And they hush when you turn, as if it were nothing.

What's being wasted from day to day
is not the dead, but is those
patches of the non-existent, lime or ashes
ready to become light and movement.
                                        Don't
be in doubt, – the sea's strength assails me –
speak they will.

FROM
Variable Star
(1981)

THOSE THOUGHTS OF YOURS OF CALAMITY

and catastrophe
in the house where you have
come to live, already
occupied
by the idea of having come
here to die
– and these who smile at you, friends,
surely this time
you're dying, they know it, and that's why
they're smiling.

IN AN EMPTY HOUSE

Should they ever come back to life. They appear to
from room to room, don't ever
come back really in this rainy air. It has
come back to life – me suddenly a seer in the slow
    brightening –
that host of buttercups and daisies outside.
Provided *there were*.

Provided there were a story anyway
– and meanwhile in the papers Munich at first light
ah thank goodness: they'd reached an agreement –
provided there were a story, exquisite amid swastikas
one September in the rain.

Today *we are* – and anyway we are bad,
part of the evil you yourself should sun and lawn turn
    overcast or no.

PLACE OF WORK

Those steps at the stairway's elbow, all
those people gone past (and passed again each day:
for work) turning from the stairs, from life.
                                                Worn out
by those reiterators, the carpet at that point,
in a cold reflection of light. Be it winter or summer
                                      and there it grows chill
in the ambush of a thought for ever like itself
ever foreseen for that same point
ever thought just the same
the glance that falls there without fail
on each day at each hour
of years of work light years
of cold – as ever
an autumn is beginning there.

WORKS IN PROGRESS

    I

It will be because lives like dead leaves do exist –
the house amidst the waters
                              plainly in ruins
that leprosy repressed by the steel
those cobwebs of barely yesterday's domestic sounds
(*the beds lying empty, the couches damp, the chairs unused*)   WCW
leave it in the flash of its enigma
expunged from traffic, reoffered at each rolling of
    Riverside Drive

don't ask yourself what's happened to them
don't say life's incineration or divorce
(but strange that of an entire metropolis you remember
    only this)

or else trifles of a winter's journey in the vastness –
flicker of the jet in its mutant's flutter
when still it is and is no more
a number-light leaping on the New York data screen

or even those signs daubed in entrance halls of ant hills –
leafy plagues on walls, on tiles, wallpapers,
what are the little swastikas doing here in the Bronx,
there were many – they say – are any number among
    doves and hawks
but you can also take them for old emblems, Indian motifs,
however they fork in this half-sleep:
drapes and banners trodden down in Europe
or the Indios' shadow without hope among skyscrapers?
Others are on their way in the agony or rapture,
new shadows disturb me that glimpsing I don't see.

II

For some I know it's not enough
to wish me dead. They hope for this:
me dead, but in disgrace.
They don't know I've done worse,
have miniaturized them in memory.

But these ones here are leaves,
trifles, signs that work full-scale,
not those frozen in miniature those incompetent
minute mouths voicing under glass
– and they'd be right if only they knew –
cramped for ever in the cast,
fossils in live cement.

III

Inopportune futile untimely
the imp of the above.

Another leaps up and annuls it
beating a different wing from down there
from the sea if sea it is that grey
of non-existence round Ellis Island
once quarantine islet
blurring in memory's cloud:
of the young Charlie
Chaplin and how many with him,
on the waiting list with him
knocking at the States' doors
with, before them, all America
soon overwhelmed in those
first stories of his
of quickest shadows
of emigrants, kitchen-boys, tramps
– and the stubborn ever in search of gold,
they'd like to make it, to form again today
with the puffings of smoke from underground
against the dimmed windows
over the frozen, over the empty in Wall Street here
one Sunday.

New York, 1967

INTERIOR

Enough of the blows enough. In the open
for a whole afternoon we flayed each other.
Call it a draw.
The hills are enveloped in wind. Already
others do battle out there, it's the turn
of the young branches hurling themselves at the panes,
of the heather, the sage in waves
always thicker and more turbid,
soon a single tide.
You call this peace? To draw near
a wood fire,
the dying taste of the bread,
the wine's transparency
where thoughtfully the day
is rekindled, just now gone down
over the cliffs with the cry of plateaus
in the fleece of precipices, the velvet
of false distances, until sleep seizes us?

OF CUTS AND STITCHES

           The toy,
sheep or lamb you patch
at the little one's command,
more strong-headed than you'd think
from its sheepish nature
is one of your family. Your profile
obstinate, resewing the toy
and that strong head: patient
with impatience – and your frowning
that yet doesn't ease its grip
on my life which goes via butterflies
and precipices... For every
scratch a stitch, for every tear
a patch.
           What value
has a needlewoman's
labour, what value
has your life?

March, 1961

REVIVAL

'Bella *L'Opzione*' – the small Jew
greets me, brisk in the wind,
come back to editing his classics.

Bellissimaaa . . .
It's repeated in echoes to encourage
or deride me
by the balcony of crows high above
hoisted up by that same wind
in the freezing, in the grey.

Among what remains of rubble
and all this stuff for building
in glass, concrete, steel,
fine place for talks and meetings.
And grimaces, sarcasm from windows to windows
that give onto nothing
from frontages threatened with collapse,
from doors that have nothing behind them,
cast me back
across twenty years
into a Venice piazza
on the jerky air of the Third Man theme
as from instants reversed in a replay,
the television ghost's rearing – . . .
                                        here it is again
the rain
cold on the cold war, the face
once loved a few moments
quickly cut away
behind a drop-curtain of tears.

GIOVANNA AND THE BEATLES

In the house's stubborn silence, in the quiet
thinking herself unheeded and alone
she breathes life into those revenants once more.
Leaving along a groove of dust
splinters of sound behind them,
between astounded walls
in a crackling they go,
the oh so lovable Beetles.

Her moment gone with theirs already?

How often at interchanges, at crossings of life
born out of nothing under music's guise
unawares, a subtle devil,
a stealthy bringer of shivers reappears
– and a hillside blazes again with green,
a sea is filled with movement –
unfailing seducer until
he's overcome and, with him, us by other musics.

EACH TIME THAT ALMOST

in secret I come back to Luino
on the lakeside piazza
spurting from a shop runs
someone to embrace me
mumbling my mother's name.
An elder brother of his years ago
did the same
and as then now suddenly
blossomed from a wall of clay
backwards along the chain
of the dead a hand is clutching out at us.

NICCOLÒ

Fourth of September, today
one dear to me dies and with him courtesy
once more and maybe this for ever.

I was with others a last time in the sea
astonished that over so many clear ghostings
a vast, definitive cloud wouldn't settle
over all the sky, but just a blur of vapour
put itself between us, powder
left behind from the summer
(there he was, you sensed, everywhere on earth and sea
straining to reach us, to break
the whitening diaphragm).
No use searching for you on further shores
all along the coast pressing on to that one
called the Beach of the Dead to know you won't come.

                                                So now
the world empties of you and the poets'
false-true *you* replenishes with you
I know now who was missing in the amaranth halo
what and who deserted the waters
of some ten days ago
already with suspicions of September. All search
   abandoned,
the names withdraw behind things,
and say no, they say no, the oleanders
stirred in the breeze.

                       And then we're back
to the sphere of the heavens, but isn't it

the usual hendiadys of sky and sea?
So stay with me, you like it here,
and heed me, you know how.

1971

NOCTURNE

Someone is plotting against you below:
the seamless ineluctable
of crickets and the starry
meadow of the shades.

It doesn't want you expatriates you
frees itself of you
refusal of refusals
the majesty of night.

MADRIGAL TO NEFERTITI

Where will it be, with whom the smile
which seems if it touches me
to know all about me,
past, future, but is oblivious of the present
should I attempt to tell her what waters
for me it becomes between palms and dunes
and emerald shores
– and she turns it back onto a yesterday
of enchantments, remnants, smoke
or postpones it until a tomorrow
which will not belong to me
and of something quite other if I speak to her, speaks?

REQUIEM

Flattened the irony, washed out the courage,
the courage done for, gaiety injured.
So then so therefore it's you
who's speaking to me
from beneath the cascade of leafage and flowers,
actually you that replies?
                                  Oh the vestments
of beauty, the adornments of death ...
with a smile or a sneer
with what face underneath that mask?

FIRST FEAR

Every corner or alley, every moment's good
for the killer who's been stalking me
night and day for years.
Shoot me, shoot me – I tell him
offering myself to his aim
in the front, the side, the back –
let's get it over with, do me in.
And saying it I realize
I'm talking to myself alone.
                                        But
it's no use, it's no use. On my own
I cannot bring myself to justice.

SECOND FEAR

There's nothing terrifying
about the voice that beckons me
and no one else
from the street below my home
at some hour of night:
it's a wind's brief wakening,
a fleeting shower.
In speaking my name it doesn't list
my misdeeds, rebuke me for my past.
With tenderness (Vittorio,
Vittorio) it disarms me, is arming
me myself against me.

OTHER PLACE OF WORK

You don't mean to tell me that you
are you or that I am I.
We went by as the years go by.
Here there is nothing of us but the specimen
or rather the image self-perpetuating
for nothing –
and waters contemplate us and windows,
think of us in the future: headlong into then,
ever fainter postscripts
vague multiples of us as we'll have been.

Autumn 1975

THE DISEASE OF THE ELM

If it matters to you it's still summer
look here how on the river-bank the tree
flakes its weaker leaves:
rosy-yellow petals of unknown flowers
– and to future memory
the evergreens motionless.

But it matters more the people step gaily,
the city rush to the river and a seagull,
ventured as far as here, be unleafed
in a flare of brilliant white.

Lead me, variable star, as long as you're able . . .

– and the day casts the banks in honey and gold
and recasts them in an oily dark
until the teeming of the lights.
                                    It darts
out from that swarm,
the humming atom, hits me
with unswerving aim
where it most stings and burns.

Come near to me, speak to me, tenderness,
– I say turning back towards
a life until yesterday close to me
today so remote – drive out
from me the insistent thorn,
the memory:
it is never satisfied.

It's finished – that shadow
murmurs a reply
in the last light – sleep now, rest.

                                          You've
removed the thorn, but not
its burning – I sigh as I give myself up to her
in dreams with her already falling.

UPHILL

'In short, existence doesn't exist'
(the other: 'read some poets,
they'll tell you
not existing exists').
That comic dialogue descended
an alleyway or two
downhill towards the sea.
Do they hold such conversations
in the worst heat of the day,
the *y'know* boys? – I asked myself
scuffing through those rockfalls – .
It has no sense at all
unless for some bitter passers-by
when entire pieces of nature
are stamped in them forever
freezing themselves in the pupils.
                                      But I
was the passer-by, it was me,
perplexed though not exactly bitter.

IN PARMA WITH A. B.

    I

Green vapour tree
at the margins of a city.
A vaporous green.
                    What other?
I'd like to be other. To be you.
For a long time a long time ago
I'd have liked to be like you
the poet of this city.
With passionate reasons then.
At that time unrequited (you
who pass not seeing me).
Knowing nothing other
to say today that shock of green
becomes immovable sorrow.

    II

If I say lit window
if I say avenue drenched with rain
it's nothing, not even a song.
Even for me my evening in Parma
would have had voice were I you
and not
half-hidden in the mind
a theme of scented dust and rain
between spring and summer.
And were it a door giving on to other doors
as far as that one walled up down there
which sooner or later will open?
Other sorrow. In spasms.

III

Half-asleep beyond that door.
It happens. Sometimes.
That to me another speaks of me
even into me.
The old tramway descended
from Marzolara to Parma
whistled a long time grazing the Baccanelli
saluting you not there
uttered the certainty, horror of the end
and that great summer sky grew convinced.

To this shadow the horror of that emptiness returns.

IV

Divine egoist, I know it is futile
asking for help from you,
I know you'd fend me away.

Hold it dear to you – he says – this
green shadow and this ache. Evasive,
moving aside he conceals it
with one of his acacia leaves –
                              invitation
to a feast which is prepared for us
shifting like a cloud
upon the shoulder of the Apennines.

AUTOSTRADA DELLA CISA

Ten years more, not even that,
before my father dies again in me
(rudely he was lowered down
and a bank of fog divided us for ever).

Today a kilometer from the pass
a tousled long-haired fury
flaps a rag from the edge of a drop
does for a day already done, and farewell.

Be sure – one leaving said to me –
sure that it doesn't finish here,
from instant to instant believe in that other life,
from slope to slope await it, it will come
as a summer may return from the far side of the gap.

So the recidivist hope speaks, bites
in a water-melon summer's pulp
sees down there those trees perpetuate
each in itself its own nymph
and behind the radiating of mirages and echoes
a lake's tremor in the parched plain
makes of Mantua a Tenochtitlán.

From tunnel to tunnel, bedazzlement to blindness
I extend a hand. It returns to me empty.
I reach out an arm, embrace a shoulder of air.

And do you still not realize
– she hisses in the tunnel's roar,
the sybil, the one
who more and more wishes to die –

do you still not suspect
that of all the colours the strongest
the most fast
is the colour of nothingness?

RIMBAUD

written on a wall

Come for an instant the sting of his name
the trickling drop from his name
inscribed in clear letters on that scorching wall.

Then he would despise me
the man with soles of wind
for having believed it.

But the shadow whether fox or rat
haunter of mastabas
darting away from under our gaze
unrelated, oblivious of us in that sinking light . . .

You'd thought of it as well.

Vanished. Slipped off to his home
of stones and sliding sand
when the desert starts to live again,
it hurls back at us that name in a lasting shudder.

Luxor, 1979

PROGRESS

Those brown eyes of hers gilded in final sun.
Illumined at a stroke beside her
the city is empurpled,
coloured topaz, emerald.

At such ostentation from the old photo laughs
the dream of the lamplighter
askew on his bicycle as though
at his touch alone an entire city
were irradiated
simultaneous with a century's lights
and all of us made to appear in her
– stump of flame now
smouldering down in her ashes.

ANOTHER BIRTHDAY

At the end of July when
from under pergolas of a bar in San Siro
amongst railings and arches you glimpse
some wedge of the sun-filled stadium
when the great empty bowl amazes
mirroring wasted time and it seems
that exactly there a year comes to die
and no one knows what else another year prepares
let us pass over this threshhold once more
so long as your heart withstand those city floodings
and a slate multiply the summer's colour.

Notes

Notes on the poems have been kept to a minimum useful for clarifying the text or its context. Dates given in square brackets to the poems from *Frontier* are those provided by the author in the contents list of the book's 1966 edition. They have been placed beneath the text here as it is not customary in English editions to give dates on the contents page. Other dates to the poems are those included by the author at the foot of his text. As Sereni explains, the dates to *Frontier* are those of composition, whereas in *Algerian Diary* they refer to the moment or occasion of the poem. In his note to *The Human Implements*, Sereni points out that rigorous dating of the poems would be merely arbitrary. However, he indicates that the poems in the present selection from 'Via Scarlatti' to 'Six in the Morning' are from 1945 to 1957, those from 'Discovery of Hatred' to 'Appointment at an Unusual Hour' are from 1958 to 1960, while those from 'A Dream' to 'The Beach' date from 1961 to 1965. The edition of Vittorio Sereni's poems used for these translations is *Tutte le poesie* edited by Maria Teresa Sereni, Mondadori, 1986.

From **Frontier**

STORM AT SALSOMAGGIORE   *page 35*

Salsomaggiore is a spa town in Emilia-Romagna, not far from Parma.

TO M. L. PASSING ABOVE HER TOWN
IN AN EXPRESS TRAIN   *page 36*

M. L. is Maria Luisa Bonfanti, whom Sereni met at university in Milan and married in 1940; her town is Parma. Sereni's original of 'the beaming lands' alludes to the myth of Phaeton, son of Helios, who was thrown into the river Po by Apollo.

DIANA   *page 37*

This poem is also addressed to his future wife. The Navigli are a series of canals connecting the river Ticino with Milan.

3 DECEMBER   *page 39*

The poem remembers Antonia Pozzi, a poet Sereni met at university in Milan. She committed suicide, and her body was discovered in fields on the outskirts of Milan towards Chiaravalle on 3 December 1938. She was twenty-six. He alludes to her poem 'La porta che si chiude' (The Closing Door) whose last stanza reads:

> And then, with lips sealed,
> with eyes open
> on the mysterious sky of shadow,
> there will be
> – you know it –
> peace.

WINTER IN LUINO   *page 41*

Luino, Sereni's birthplace, is on Lake Maggiore close to the Swiss frontier. The 'coal-heaps jagged in the sun' were to fuel steam engines on the railway line crossing the border. Originally Luino was intended to be on the main line, but Chiasso subsequently became the more important frontier station. Zenna and Creva, which occur in the titles of poems following, are place names near Luino.

From **Algerian Diary**

BELGRADE   *page 56*

' – the Danube! the Sava! – ' is a late addition to the poem, only in the 1979 edition, and put there Sereni explained because of critical confusion about the two 'chimeras' in the poem which signify these rivers. Giosuè Bonfanti is a literary critic and friend of the poet.

DIMITRIOS   *page 58*

The poem is dedicated to Maria Teresa Sereni, b. 24 July 1941.

THE ATHENIAN GIRL   *page 59*

'despinís' is the Greek for 'girl'; 'Kaidari' is a suburb of Athens where part of the Pistoia Division was encamped during the summer of 1942, waiting to reinforce the Axis armies in North Africa. As the note of places and times at the end of this poem indicates, the first two sections refer to Sereni's situation before, the second two after his capture.

ALGERIAN DIARY   *page 61*

Remo Valianti was one of Sereni's fellow-prisoners.

In part 7, the 'frail hedgerow' is a reminiscence of Leopardi's 'L'Infinito' and the 'German crowd' an allusion to Dante's *Inferno* XVI, line 5.

THE AFRICAN SICKNESS   *page 73*

Giansiro Ferrata, a literary critic, was a friend of Sereni. 'Bidonville' is a French word meaning 'shanty town'. 'Barracans' are a type of Arab clothing. The 'Isle of the Sards' is Sardinia, alluded to in this form because the original adapts line 104 of Canto VI, the Ulysses Canto, in Dante's *Inferno*.

In *Tutte le poesie* this poem appears twice: in the *Algerian Diary* and also in *The Human Implements* between, in this selection, 'The Lines' and 'The Alibi and the Benefit'. While its placement in the latter book better conforms with the date and style of the poem's composition, its subject matter is continuous with the rest of *Algerian Diary*.

SEPTEMBER THE EIGHTH   *page 77*

On 8 September 1943 General Badoglio, head of Italy's government after the fall of Mussolini on 25 July, signed a separate armistice with the Allies. '*Sale macaroni*' (Dirty Italians) is a jibe by French-speaking Algerians at Sereni and his fellow prisoners of war.

From **The Human Implements**

Via Scarlatti   *page 81*

The Serenis lived at 27 Via Scarlatti, Milan from 1946 to 1952. The poem made its first appearance in the 1947 edition of *Diario d'Algeria*; its form is modelled on poems by Umberto Saba such as 'Città vecchia' from *Trieste e una donna* (1912).

The Misapprehension   *page 83*

The poem recalls Baudelaire's sonnet 'A une passante' from *Les Fleurs du mal*.

Those Children Playing   *page 91*

Sereni frequently heard Umberto Saba repeat the aphorism quoted in italics, which is not to be found in any of his poems.

Saba   *page 92*

Umberto Saba (1883–1957) was a Triestine poet and friend of Sereni. He spent much of his time in Milan between 1946 and 1948. The 18th of April 1948 is the day on which the Communists and Socialists of the *Fronte popolare* were defeated by the Christian Democrats in the first elections for the new Italian Republic.

Situation   *page 94*

In an attempt to clarify this particularly enigmatic poem, Sereni informed the translators that it might be entitled 'Jealousy'.

Appointment at an Unusual Hour   *page 96*

'the stolen fox ...' alludes to the story related by Montaigne in *Essays* I.XIV derived from Plutarch's *Life of Lycurgus* 18.

In Sleep   *page 98*

In this poem Sereni alludes to 25 April 1945, the end of the Second World War, to the post-war reconstruction, and again to 8 September 1943, when General Badoglio signed a separate peace with the Allies.

The 'compulsory ranks of how many pre-militarized Sundays' in part I refers to what was called the Fascist Sunday when citizens were required to take part in para-military activities.

'Pantalones' in part IV refers to the figure from the *Commedia dell'arte*, Harlequin's master, greedy and mean, but who is perpetually tricked into paying by his more cunning and less honest servant.

The italicized lines in part VI are from a popular song of the time called 'In cerca di te' (In Search of You).

THE ALIBI AND THE BENEFIT   *page 103*

Luciano Erba (1922–) is a Milanese poet. 'Il Tempo di Milano', a Milanese newspaper, could also mean: the weather in Milan.

POETRY IS A PASSION?   *page 104*

The Drina is a river, and Larissa a town, in Yugoslavia. The 'summer of iron' is 1942. The lines in italics are from Gabriele d'Annunzio (1863–1938). Sereni cites lines 131–2 and 194 of 'Il novilunio' from *L'Alcyone* (1903).

ON THE CREVA ROAD AGAIN   *page 108*

The poem alludes to Leopardi's 'Amore e morte'.

ON A CEMETERY PHOTOGRAPH   *page 110*

The original of the italicized line, '*O dormiente, che cosa è sonno?*' is by Leonardo da Vinci from the *Codice Atlantico*, and continues 'Il sonno ha similitudine colla morte' (Sleep has a likeness to death).

From **Variable Star**

IN AN EMPTY HOUSE   *page 122*

The poem makes an allusion to the Munich agreement of 29 September 1938.

PLACE OF WORK   *page 123*

The poem is set in the old Mondadori offices in central Milan.

WORKS IN PROGRESS   *page 124*

I: '*the beds lying empty . . .*' reproduces two lines from 'These' by William Carlos Williams. Sereni's translation of the poem appears on pp. 342–3 of *Tutte le poesie*.

III: Ellis Island was the quarantine island for immigrants, the symbolic and official gateway for millions of future citizens of the USA, from 1892–1954, when it was closed. The little island has now become a historical monument, joining the not distant Statue of Liberty.

REVIVAL   *page 129*

L'Opzione (The Option) is the title of a story by Sereni set in and around the Frankfurt Book Fair.

GIOVANNA AND THE BEATLES   *page 130*

Giovanna is the Serenis' third daughter. The Beatles were humorously known in Italy by the mistranslation 'Gli Scarafaggi' (The Beetles).

NICCOLÒ   *page 132*

The poem is an elegy to the literary critic Niccolò Gallo. 'The poets' false-true *you*' refers to Eugenio Montale's 'Il tu', the first poem in *Satura* (1971).

NOCTURNE   *page 134*

This poem and the following ('Madrigal to Nefertiti') are two parts from the sequence 'I Translated Char'. Sereni describes the group of poems in his author's note as 'moments of life, or better, recoveries (not exercises, not "studies") related to the time when I was occupied on that work.'

OTHER PLACE OF WORK   *page 139*

The poem is set in the new Mondadori offices at Segrate, a modern complex of buildings in countryside beyond the suburbs of Milan.

UPHILL   *page 142*

'The *y'know* boys' is an attempt to transpose 'i ragazzi Cioè' into English, where the original refers to the use of the word 'cioè' ('that's to say') compulsively, like a verbal tic, in young people's talk.

IN PARMA WITH A. B.   *page 143*

A. B. is Attilio Bertolucci (1911–). The Baccanelli is a district of Parma.

AUTOSTRADA DELLA CISA   *page 145*

Sereni's note to this poem reads: 'The stretch in question is from La Spezia to Parma in the direction of the Po valley. "Tenochtitlán", the capital of the Aztec empire before the Spanish conquest, today Mexico City, was blessed with a lake: city warm to the memory as always since the catastrophe.'

RIMBAUD   *page 147*

Sereni's note reads: 'Anyone who has visited the temple of Luxor would have been able to see that writing. There exist, as far as I know, no proofs of, or documents about a journey there of the "Homme aux semelles de vent", in any case, improbable that he wrote it. *Mastaba* is the modern name given to ancient pyramid-shaped Egyptian burial chambers in stone.'

PROGRESS   *page 148*

The poem's concluding lines refer to the suicides transformed into trees in Dante's *Inferno* XIII, line 26.

ANOTHER BIRTHDAY   *page 149*

San Siro is an area of Milan where the Meazza Football Stadium is situated.

*Some Contemporary Poets in Translation
from Anvil*

BEI DAO
The August Sleepwalker
Translated by Bonnie S. McDougall

ANA BLANDIANA
The Hour of Sand
Translated by Peter Jay and Anca Cristofovici

ELISABETH BORCHERS
Fish Magic
Translated by Anneliese Wagner

NINA CASSIAN
Life Sentence
Edited by William Jay Smith

IVAN V. LALIĆ
The Passionate Measure
Translated by Francis R. Jones

JÁNOS PILINSZKY
The Desert of Love
Translated by János Csokits and Ted Hughes

YANNIS RITSOS
Exile and Return
Translated by Edmund Keeley

SÁNDOR WEÖRES
Eternal Moment
Edited by Miklós Vajda
Translated by Edwin Morgan, William Jay Smith and others

THE POETRY OF SURVIVAL
Post-War Poets of Central and Eastern Europe
Edited by Daniel Weissbort

*A full catalogue is available
from the publisher*